E·S·S·E·N·T·I·A·L·L·Y
YUGOSLAVIA

ALSO AVAILABLE IN THE *ESSENTIALLY* SERIES

Essentially Turkey
Carole and Chris Stewart

by the same author
The Adriatic Islands and Corfu (1971)
Celia Irving

E·S·S·E·N·T·I·A·L·L·Y
YUGOSLAVIA

Suština Jugoslavije

CELIA IRVING

CHRISTOPHER HELM
London

© 1988 Celia Irving

Line drawings by Mary Budd
Christopher Helm (Publishers) Ltd, Imperial House,
21–25 North Street, Bromley, Kent BR1 1SD

British Library Cataloguing in Publication Data

Irving, Celia
    Essentially Yugoslavia.
    1. Yugoslavia—Description and travel—
    Guide-books
    I. Title
    914.97′0424   DR1213

    ISBN 0–7470–1600–3

Typeset by Opus, Oxford
Printed and bound in Great Britain by
Biddles Ltd, Guildford and Kings Lynn

C·O·N·T·E·N·T·S

Foreword **vii**

Map **viii**

Introduction **1**

1. The Sea . . . the Mainland Sea **13**
2. A Chain of Islands **55**
3. Inland Yugoslavia **93**
4. Mountains and Lakes for all Seasons **133**
5. Famous Cities: Inland and on the Coast **151**
6. Practical Information **179**

Index **189**

For my family who love Yugoslavia as I do. And for all our friends in that lovely country — especially the people of Korčula where, for twenty years we have had our island home.

F·O·R·E·W·O·R·D

It was with great pleasure that I read *Essentially Yugoslavia*, which provides an excellent introduction to one of Europe's most varied and fascinating countries. More than any other British travel writer, Celia Irving is regarded with great affection and esteem in Yugoslavia. Her remarkable knowledge of the country and its people and her infectious enthusiasm combine to give her writings unusual colour and vitality. This book will win many new friends for Yugoslavia, and provide unique insight into its beauties, many of them still little-known.

Miodrag Mirivic
President of the Federal Committee for Tourism, Yugoslavia

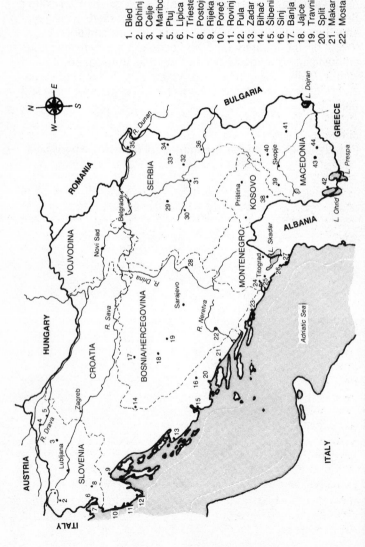

1. Bled
2. Bohinj
3. Celje
4. Maribor
5. Ptuj
6. Lipica
7. Trieste
8. Postojna
9. Rijeka
10. Poreč
11. Rovinj
12. Pula
13. Zadar
14. Bihač
15. Sibenik
16. Sinj
17. Banja Luka
18. Jajce
19. Travnik
20. Split
21. Makarska
22. Mostar
23. Dubrovnik
24. Kotor
25. Cetinje
26. Bar
27. Ulcinje
28. Višegrad
29. Kracgujevac
30. Kraljevo
31. Kruševac
32. Sokobanja
33. Gamzigrad
34. Zaječar
35. Trajan's Tablet
36. Niš
37. Peć
38. Prizren
39. Tetova
40. Kumanova
41. Stip
42. Ohrid
43. Bitola
44. Heraclea Linkestis

I·N·T·R·O·D·U·C·T·I·O·N

YUGOSLAVIA — COMPLEX, BEAUTIFUL AND INFINITELY VARIED

Yugoslavia is a country of such infinite variety that there seems ever to be a little more to see, to savour, and to experience. Set in the middle of southern Europe, between East and West, with its feet in the Mediterranean and its head in the Alps, the scenery is extraordinarily vivid and varied. Created from such very early origins, the history is complex and fascinating; and the country owes its culture to both Western and Eastern influences. Its ancient art treasures are superlative, and the people, being Slav, are warm-hearted, generous to a fault, proud, and steadfast.

When people visit Yugoslavia the experience is apt to develop into a love affair: if they like it there are no half measures. And, whether they go for the warm Adriatic Sea and the clear skies, for the lakes and mountains that abound, for a view of the priceless Byzantine buildings, frescoes and icons, or a tour that will show them the different influences of both East and West in this complex land, there will always be surprises. Each visit will uncover a new experience; something more to see; someone new to meet in this country that welcomes visitors, values its freedom more than anything else on earth, and is determined to pursue its own special brand of unaligned socialism in a free world.

Yugoslavia's coastline stretches along the shores of the Adriatic Sea from Italian Trieste in the north-west to the frontier of Albania in the south-east. The entire coast is deeply indented with inlets, wide curving bays, fjords and rock-pointed channels where the sea is protected by long arms of maquis and tree-covered hills, ending up in a shallow bay with, probably, an ancient village and port basking in the sun. And, though it stretches for only 500 miles as the crow flies, it is many times longer than that in reality. The coastal road, known as the Jadranska Magistrala — the Adriatic Highway — modern though it is, has to circumnavigate inlets, fjords and cliff-edged coastal hills with many sharp turns and twists, affording superb views of the sea and islands en route. By ship the view is reversed. The water is so deep that passenger ships can stay close to the shore, threading their way through the islands as they make their way down the coast.

New building has been considerably guided by the South Adriatic Plan, drawn up in the 1960s with the help of the United Nations. The object was to ensure that, unlike what happened in countries like Spain, new development would not spoil either the original very lovely skyline along the coast, or detract from the quiet beauty of the many historically important settlements and ports. The plan also included strict controls over drainage systems, sewage and purification plants. It is these measures that have helped to keep the Yugoslav side of the Adriatic Sea one of the least polluted in Europe. The water is translucently clear to a depth of many metres.

The entire Yugoslav coast lies in the Mediterranean area of Europe, but there are subtle differences to be detected as one travels south-east. The colours vary, and become more vivid; and the climate gets a little hotter the further south one goes.

Rather than spoil the look of the villages, and disturb their normal way of life, the tourist authorities in each region have planned hotels and complexes outside the original villages in bays where there is shallow as well as deep water, shade from trees in park land, and flat terrain near the sea for comfortable walking — often under mediterranean pines that give out such an evocative scent in the hot sun.

There are many resorts along the length of the coastline. Nearest to Italy, the first 40 km stretch is part of Slovenia. It includes the sophisticated little resort of Portorož — the Port of Roses — with its wide promenade, casino, very good hotels, and its international sculptors' symposiums which have left a park strewn with examples of the sculptor's art.

But the first of the really big holiday complexes lies a little further south of Portorož — still on the western side of the Istrian Peninsula — at Poreč, itself a very beautiful and

2

ancient settlement with many Roman and early Byzantine remains. In fact, if you are lucky, while bathing in some of the bays you may find the mosaics of Roman floors which have long since disintegrated and subsided under the sea.

Around Poreč the coast consists of tree-covered points that enclose wide protected lagoons with clear blue and emerald-green water, transparent to a remarkable depth. Almost every sport is provided in the holiday complexes at Poreč, with tuition available; not to mention barbecues, floor shows, discos, open-air dancing, and performances of folklore at night.

There are many such resorts dotted along the coast, but none is an exact copy of another. Some have shingle beaches; some, especially further south in Montenegro, have coarse sand and small coloured stones — for instance, at Budva. Here the colours are jewel-like: rosy pink, mauve, green, beige and slate-blue. The stones are small enough for children to collect and take home with them.

Shells can be found everywhere, including the huge lostura, and the shining mother-of-pearl ormars, as well as delicate many-hued sea-urchins. But the best shells are on the shore in the far south near the Albanian border, where there is a fine sandy beach that stretches for more than 8 km. Murex shells as well as the more ordinary bi-valves can be collected by the score here. The Romans valued the murex for its purple dye that they used for their Imperial togas. But just when did they first discover its properties? And who would have thought that one of the finest collections of shells in the world is housed in the crypt of a Franciscan monastery in Makarska, mid-Dalmatia?

Many hotels in Yugoslavia provide special areas in the grounds for children to play with swings and slides, mini-golf and other amusements. Children are universally loved by the Yugoslavs and nothing is too good for them. Unlike our children, they are not put to bed early in the evening but, by six pm are dressed in their best clothes, and paraded in their prams with their elder brothers and sisters through the streets and along the promenades, pushed by their parents and grandparents. This walking out of an evening and meeting with friends on the way, is a time-honoured custom in the country, particularly in the south where the evenings are warm; it is reminiscent of southern Spain.

Another time-honoured and unique Yugoslav custom is their *Baka-Servis*. *Baka* is an affectionate name for Granny; and it is taken absolutely for granted that Granny will look after the babies while parents continue with their jobs.

Baka-Servis must be one of the greatest hidden assets of this delightful and often surprising country. But there are also pre-schools and baby crèches where parents can leave their small children. These centres are called a *vrtić*, or children's garden, and are run sometimes by the school authorities, and sometimes by the local convent — as in Korčula where the Dominican nuns have a *vrtić*. They take the place of play-schools, as Yugoslav children don't normally start school before the age of six.

The most sophisticated resorts are, as might be expected, on the mainland near the more important and historic towns. In between are the holiday places which vary from the super-active always-something-to-do kind, to the quiet and sleepy. There are those specially geared for nudists — the Yugoslavs prefer to call them 'naturists'. Others are equipped with up-to-date yacht marinas.

The islands, too, offer great variety. Some are quiet, such as Cres and Pag in the north-west; Čiovo, Šolta, and Drvenik off-shore from Split; and Mljet, Koločep and Lopud near Dubrovnik. In these islands life goes on very much as it always has done with vineyards to be tended, vegetables to grow, sheep to watch over, and fish to catch. Fishing is not just a livelihood but a hobby — even a passion — with many islanders, and no Dalmatian will eat meat when he can get fresh fish. Then there are the less known and even quieter islands, such as Ugljan and Dugi Otok near Zadar; Murter near Šibenik and — perhaps the most beautiful of them all — the far-out islands of Vis and Lastovo which, for the present, remain closed to foreigners except in special circumstances. As the authorities explain, 'We have conscription for our young men (ten months to one year) so we must have somewhere to train them!'

The most popular and highly developed holiday islands are Lošinj, Rab and Krk in the north-west, and Hvar, Brač and Korčula further south-east. There is also one other island which, until now, has had no part in tourism. This is the island of Brioni, just out to sea from Pula. Brioni, complete with two large hotel buildings, was President Tito's home, when only his invited guests visited this small and very lovely place. Now it is open for both Yugoslavs and foreigners who can stay in the hotels and enjoy what was the President's favourite residence. It is a most attractive place.

An unusual way to see a lot of the coast and islands is to take a cruise on one of the informal old sailing ships which, brought up to date, sail along the coast from ports like Zadar, Split and Dubrovnik. They carry only a few passengers, serve good food, call in at some of the islands and ports, and sometimes make unscheduled stops in a particularly inviting bay. The tourist offices have details of these cruises.

Yugoslavia has warm seas and blue skies, but these are not the only things that draw people to the country. Inland, there are mountains, huge lakes, majestic upland forests and, in some cases, a combination of all three. The country's alpine borders are with Italy and Austria, and they all share the Julian and Karavanke Alps. Mount Triglav is the highest mountain in Yugoslavia and it overlooks all three countries.

For summer walking and climbing, as well as skiing in winter, there are many upland and lake centres. Just south of Zagreb in Croatia, there are the phenomenal Plitvice Lakes. Then, in the heart of Serbia, Kopaonik — 1,980 m above sea-level — is being developed for both summer and winter tourism. On a much smaller scale, in Montenegro's mountainous interior is Žabljak, a small village perched high up on a wide plateau near one of the world's deepest canyons in the Durmitor range of mountains.

For the ultimate in lakeside beauty, go to the far south to Lake Skadar, shared with Albania; or, further east, to Ohrid and its sister lakes, Prespa and Dojran, in the depths of Macedonia, bordering on Greece.

As if all this were not enough, there are many spas where a family holiday can be combined pleasurably with medical treatment.

Facilities for riding holidays can be found too; the most outstanding being at Lipica in Slovenia where the pale grey Lippizaner horses have been bred for hundreds of years.

Some of Yugoslavia's rivers are ideal for canoeing, and there is even rafting for the more intrepid! The biggest of the many rivers are the Sava and the Dunav which join forces at Belgrade to flow, as the Danube, to the Black Sea. Other famous rivers are the Drina, which runs through Bosnia, and the Neretva which emerges into the Adriatic Sea between Split and Dubrovnik. These rivers are often dramatic, flowing through gorges and canyons — each has its own attraction, and there are tales to be told about all.

There is abundant and fascinating sightseeing: outstanding buildings from the Roman period onwards through medieval and renaissance times; a great variety of national costume, folklore and festivals; and oriental areas where the people still wear Turkish dress and attend the Imams in the mosques. But, though mixed, the people are of Slav stock, with the warmth and strong feelings of all Slavs. Interested in everyone, their Slav and Balkan hospitality and friendliness are very real, particularly where British people are concerned — it is 40 years since World War II, but they still think of the British as their allies.

Another bond between English people and the Yugoslavs is their sense of humour. They, too, have an adult cynical turn of mind which adds point to their wit, and strikes a corresponding spark when they tell their sometimes rather bitter jokes about war and, more recently, the state of their economy. This last is a never-ending source of discussion. 'The trouble with us,' they will joke, 'is that we take three years to pass a new law curbing spending, and the next five years finding ways of getting round it.' Another of their jokes štems from their resistance during the last war. According to the story, a group of Tito's Partisans had managed to surround quite a sizeable detachment of the enemy and were methodically polishing them off. Suddenly, the Partisan leader called for his men to stop. 'But why?' shouted the second-in-command. 'There are still a few left alive!' 'Ah, my friend,' the captain said, 'you must learn to think ahead. After the war we shall need some tourists!'

But, though their humour may be caustic, the Yugoslav people are, above all, warmhearted in the extreme, with an overriding belief in family life and in the value of friendship. They make friends quickly with people of any nation; it is the individual that counts, not the nationality. And they welcome friends into their homes with lavish hospitality offering open-heartedly anything they happen to have. At the same time, if someone offends them, they are not easily cajoled into changing their minds. They are never obsequious. They do things for you because they want to, not because you might tip. For, more than anything else, they prize their freedom, so bitterly fought for after centuries of overlordship and repression by stronger powers from both east and west.

HISTORY

The history of the country is very complex, but to get the maximum enjoyment out of a visit to Yugoslavia, it is worth knowing a little about it. Then, the explanation for the differences in language, food, religion, ethnic characteristics, facial features, and even thought-processes, becomes simple.

Yugoslavia — meaning the land of the South Slavs — really only came into being as a country when, at the end of World War I, the different and separate states and regions were amalgamated into 'The Kingdom of Serbs, Croats and Slovenes' which title, in a rather high-handed way, failed to mention Montenegro, Bosnia-Hercegovina, a great part of Macedonia, and most of Dalmatia, all of which were also lumped in together. Before that time, all these regions were loosely termed by the West as 'part of the cock-pit of Europe' and thought of as a tiresome area, and something to do with the demise of the Ottoman Empire.

History lessons in Western schools talked vaguely about the Serbs and the Croats. It was all rather nebulous and, when some early student-nationalists shook the world by assassinating their hated overlord Ferdinand, the nephew of the Emperor Franz Josef in 1914, few people can have realised that Sarajevo was neither in Serbia nor Croatia, but in Bosnia: a separate state — and one-time medieval kingdom — which was overrun by the Ottoman Empire in 1463 after a long, fierce and cruel war. That overlordship continued until the last part of the nineteenth century when, not freedom, but the Austrian Empire took over. And the same story, with variations, obtains for the rest of the lands which now constitute Yugoslavia.

Young couriers on the coaches that transport you from airport to hotel, or from one resort to another, blithely quote one of their favourite sayings: 'Yugoslavia is a country of seven frontiers, six republics, five nations, four main religions, three languages, two alphabets, but only one Yugoslavia.' They are intensely proud of this last fact and, for the vast majority of people in the country, this is the most precious of all their assets, and achieved only in the twentieth century. Something to be guarded — if necessary fought for — at all costs.

The seven frontiers are with Italy, Austria, Hungary, Romania, Bulgaria, Greece and Albania. The six countries of the Federated States are Slovenia, Croatia, Bosnia/Hercegovina — originally Hercegovina was a separate principality — Serbia, Montenegro and Macedonia. Of these, four were at some time kingdoms: Croatia, Bosnia, Serbia and Montenegro. But for 500 years these countries were divided between east and west and subjected to completely different influences. Slovenia came under Austrian rule; Croatia under the combined Austro/Hungarian Empire; Bosnia, Hercegovina, Serbia, Montenegro and Macedonia were all under the influence of the Turkish Empire until the late nineteenth century when the Hapsburgs began to encroach further east. Complicating it all still more, the coastal lands and islands of Dalmatia — except for the medieval republic of Dubrovnik — were for centuries subject to Venice.

All these facts help to explain why there are at least four religions: Roman Catholic and Protestant in the west; and Serbian Orthodox and Muslim in the east. Apart from other deflections, the country was caught bang in the middle of the division of the Roman Empire, when those west of the dividing line received Christianity from Rome, while those to the east came under the Byzantine church of Constantinople.

These historical influences have all left their mark on Yugoslavia and made it a land of such infinite variety, not only geographically, though the natural barriers of mountains and rivers determined the early frontiers, but on the towns and villages, religious buildings, outstanding art treasures and, above all, on the people themselves. For the South Slavs, when they came from 'behind the Carpathian Mountains' to settle in this part of Europe in the seventh century integrated, by and large, with the descendents of Illyrians, Greeks and Romans. In the middle centuries there were also Venetians along the coast. While, inland, Magyars and Austrians influenced the lives, customs, food and literature of everyone under their jurisdiction. Further east the contrast was even greater. The Muslim faith was introduced, oriental dress was adopted by many, and Turkish food became the norm — as it did in Greece and Bulgaria.

The Cyrillic alphabet, too, created by saints Cyril and Methodius with their disciples, Kliment and Naum, in the ninth century, was adopted in the east of the country, while the latin alphabet became universal in place of the older Glagolitic script in the west.

THE REGIME

Before they arrive and can see for themselves, it is difficult for first-time visitors to know what to expect in the way of rules and regulations, both for the inhabitants and for themselves. I have met people apprehensive of what they will find; fearful that they are going to a police state with a regimented population where hotels and everything else is state owned.

The present constitution of Yugoslavia is one of the most liberal, though still one-party, forms of socialism — or communism with a small 'c' — in existence. President Tito, who broke off relations with Stalin and the communist bloc in 1948, was determined that his country should enjoy full and unaligned independence. Yugoslavia is not, contrary to some misconceptions, a member of the Comintern, or the Warsaw Pact. Tito was also dedicated to complete decentralisation, so that the Federal government can only advise, passing laws which each republic in the federation can question and even adapt, according to local requirements, so long as it doesn't affect the country's security. In some cases the law is

*President Tito who created modern Yugoslavia after leading his
people to victory in World War Two*

interpreted at local commune level and varied according to
that commune's special needs.

Virtually nothing is state run, or directly administered, with
the exception of the armed forces, the Foreign Office, the
Home Office and the Yugoslav National Bank (the equivalent
of the Bank of England). Other banks work in rivalry with one
another while firms and joint enterprises — in tourism and in
industry — carry on their business in a considerably cut-throat
manner. The biggest difference between Yugoslavia's business precepts and those of capitalist countries is that there are
no absentee shareholders. All profits, after state tax, are
ploughed back into the business, with the exception of yearly
bonuses which are shared by all members of the firm. The
exact amount of the bonus is decided by vote at one of the
statutory meetings which must be held by joint committees of
management and workforce every year. Arguments can be
fierce (Yugoslavs like to get the best for their families!) but a
good compromise is usually reached to ensure that enough of
the profits is available for the future expansion of the firm.
Yugoslav citizens can invest their savings in state projects,
such as road development, and receive a fixed return on their
money, but the difference in salary between directors and

shop-floor employees is far less than it is in the West; and it is written into the constitution that workers' committees must be involved in management decisions.

Unlike Eastern Bloc countries, there is a good deal of unemployment in Yugoslavia, particularly among those graduating at universities and medical schools, though the latter could be directed profitably to out-of-the-way areas instead of staying (as is their wish) in the large cities, were the regime less liberal!

Many Yugoslavs go abroad to work, sometimes for years at a time but — as with all Slavs — the pull of their homeland calls them back in the end, and it is commonplace to meet older men and women who speak English with a Canadian, Australian, New Zealand or American accent. They have returned to their family homes, to live on comfortable foreign currency pensions.

The family house and the land that goes with it are sacrosanct. Yugoslavs own both freehold and soil, as we do in the West. They can also own foreign currency or dinar savings accounts on which they receive interest. They also spend a good deal on improving and adding on to their homes.

Unlike the Eastern Bloc countries, Yugoslavs keep their passports permanently in their pockets — just as we do — and, except for a handful who have engaged in subversive action, they are free to cross frontiers at will. There is a comprehensive social security system and a health service which is free except for a very small charge on medicines prescribed.

Many small restaurants and guest houses are owned and run privately. Any family can apply for a licence to start a small private business, and can now employ ten, sometimes twenty permanent and even more seasonal workers (according to the type of business) once they obtain that licence; new legislation having increased the number from the former maximum of five. But such businesses are fairly heavily taxed, partly to prevent a surge of capitalism, and also to protect the provision in the constitution that no man shall wax rich by the exploitation of others.

Quite new in Yugoslavia (1985) is the law allowing foreign partners to obtain over 50 per cent participation in a business — including tourist projects — together with a considerable relaxation of the rules governing such ventures. Although foreign firms have been able in the past to participate in up to 49 per cent of the total investment for certain major projects, there were sizeable restrictions. These have now been very much eased.

There is now completely new legislation to allow for time-sharing. This radical change, both for foreign tourist firms and for the individual holidaymaker who likes to feel he is in his own home abroad, opens up many new possibilities.

Yugoslavia, in under 40 years, has become a modern twentieth-century country. She has oil, gold, silver, copper, aluminium and iron among other natural wealth. Shipbuilding, clothing, leatherwear, knitwear and agricultural produce and wines are among her exports. But perhaps her most important foreign currency earner is tourism. And, in the country's current 1987–91 five-year plan, tourism and agriculture are the two most important items.

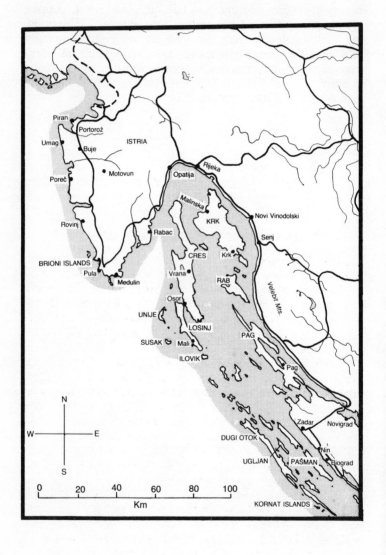

Piran
Portorož
Umag
Buje
ISTRIA
Motovun
Poreč
Rijeka
Opatija
Malinska
Rovinj
KRK
Novi Vinodolski
Rabac
Senj
BRIONI ISLANDS
CRES
Krk
Pula
Vrana
RAB
Medulin
Osor
Velebit Mts.
UNIJE
LOSINJ
SUSAK
Mali
PAG
ILOVIK
Pag
Zadar
Novigrad
DUGI OTOK
Nin
UGLJAN
PAŠMAN
Biograd

N
W — E
S

0   20   40   60   80   100
Km

KORNAT ISLANDS

C·H·A·P·T·E·R · 1
The Sea....the Mainland Sea

Istria, Primorje and Northern Dalmatia

Though warm, and with many hours of sunshine both in summer and winter, this north-west area of the Yugoslav coast is not normally quite so hot as it is farther south. There are more deciduous trees interspersed with the pines and the maquis, and the sea may be a degree or two cooler than in the deep south. All the towns of the Istrian peninsula are served by the airport of Pula.

The biggest seaside resorts here are Poreč, Umag, Pula itself, Rovinj and Rabac. Poreč has one of the longest established complete holiday complexes with everything you can think of provided in the way of entertainment. There are the renowned Green and Blue lagoons; lovely woods — with nightingales in summer — shallow bays for children; plenty of night-life; and hotel buses taking guests into the town. It is worth seeing the old town of Poreč whether you are staying there, or in another resort in the area.

A Roman *castrum* in the second century, Poreč was an important port which had already been populated in prehistoric times. The present layout of the streets still shows the outlines of the *castrum*; the *decumanus* is still the main street of the town; and there remain traces of the Forum, with some of the original paving. The present houses on this paving rely only on its sturdiness — they have no other foundations! There are the remains of a temple of Neptune and another, it is

13

The sixth-century Basilica of St Euphrasius shelters the remains of an even earlier church

thought, of Mars. But the most outstanding of all the buildings is the beautiful sixth-century Basilica of St Euphrasius which stands on a much earlier fourth-century basilica whose mosaic floors are several feet below the present level of the church and can be viewed through an opening in the floor above. The great glory of the basilica is its huge murals in gold and mother-of-pearl mosaic, reminiscent of the mosaics in Ravenna. But it is the chapel and original baptistry — to one side of the main aisles of the present basilica — that gives one that extraordinary feeling of passing back through time to the days of the early Christian martyrs and their hard-won freedom to worship through such terrible tribulations — especially in this area, so close to Imperial Rome. This earlier church was begun in about AD 313, the very year in which the Emperor Diocletian — that zealous destroyer of Christian heretics — died further south in Split (see Chapter 5).

North of Poreč are the quieter resorts of Umag in a flat area which is very good for young children and — the other side of

Portorož and almost on the Italian border — Koper and Ankaran.

Medieval Piran, close to Portorož, is an enchanting small town with a fascinating museum, a beautiful little statue of the seventeenth-century violinist and composer Tartini, and the house in which he was born. Facing the harbour is another baroque house, a delightful extravaganza of a 'Venetian Palace' built — it is said — by a sea captain for his mistress. In defiance of the town's shocked criticism he vowed she should have the grandest house in Piran.

Inland, in the wine-growing area (*Malvazia* and *Cabernet*, in particular), are three fortified hill villages well worth visiting. These are Motovun, Buje and Pazin — all photogenic in the extreme. Pazin has one of the best preserved medieval fortresses in the country.

South of Poreč is Vrsar, on the outer edge of the Lim Fjord, where oysters are cultivated. Vrsar has stayed a very sleepy relaxed sort of village with a tourist complex just up the hill that has long catered for naturists.

Then comes Rovinj, in some ways reminiscent of Piran, an attractive port with a big harbour bobbing with small craft, overlooked by the huge church of St Euphemia up on the hill.

A sumptuous extravaganza built by a sea captain for his love!

St Euphemia's statue acts as a weather-cock at the top of the very tall spire and, in the days of sailing ships, sailors would watch her to see if she was welcoming them into port, or had turned her back on them — in which case the winds made it unsafe for the ships to make landfall. Again at Rovinj, the holiday hotels are built away from the port, one of them on a small island.

At the southern tip of the Istrian Peninsula close to Pula (see Chapter 5) is the small village of Medulin. For families with young children, this gentle place, away from the bustle of Pula, has become a favourite spot. The pine trees grow on flat sandy spits of land just above sea level, giving natural shade when the sun is high.

On Istria's eastern shore, and facing the island of Cres, lies Rabac with its huge lighthouse, sheltered fishing village, large holiday hotels and auto-camping site. Rabac is particularly warm and sheltered, with thickly wooded hills leading up to Labin where, though the new town is too industrial to be beautiful, the old fortified Venetian town higher up is worth visiting, not just for its attractive architecture, but for the Venetian coal mine — now a museum — in the mountain. From Rabac the coastal bus service runs efficiently in either direction so that visiting other parts of Istria, or heading north along the Kvarner Bay to Opatija and Rijeka (see Chapter 5) is easy.

Rijeka's international airport is actually on the island of Krk, reached from the mainland these days by a spectacular bridge. Until 1980 a hard working — almost non-stop — ferry, piled up with cars and coaches, crossed the narrow strip of water. Krk airport also serves many smaller and lesser known resorts — like Moščenička Draga, an almost unpronounceable name, Kraljevica, Crikvenica, Novi Vinodolski and Senj. These last four towns had strong medieval connections with the all-powerful Princes of Krk — the Frankopans. All four towns have castles, and early Roman remains. Novi Vinodolski was the place where the Vinodol Code was drawn up. This was an early Croatian Common Law document written in the medieval Glagolitic script of Croatia in 1288 — a kind of Domesday Book for the rights of the people.

Senj owes much of its earlier fame to the pirates who lived in the town during Venetian and Turkish times. These expert sailors of Senj would watch the weather and the big trading ships of the two rich powers and, when the moment was right, would attack and plunder. Though pirates, these local boys were looked on as heroes fighting against the oppressors; a fact testified to by many heroic ballads.

16

THE SEA . . . THE MAINLAND SEA

All four towns can accommodate people who want a really relaxed holiday by the sea. And at Crikvenica there is also a clinic with modern equipment for chest ailments.

At Zadar (see Chapter 5) the military airport has now been enlarged to take international commercial traffic, bringing within reach some fascinating and extremely early old villages and settlements, as well as an attractive and rather different part of the coast. In this area the coastal mountains recede further inland to give a wide flat plain bordering the sea. This plain is extremely fertile and was obviously, in early days, easier to defend.

As well as being ideal for holidays — with its sea protected by an almost unbroken line of islands — history has left its mark on the area. For instance Novigrad, set on an inland sea, is quiet, sleepy, and particularly warm in summer. It is a lovely small place to stay in for anybody motoring in the country. There was a Roman town in the area and, from the sixth century, a bishopric. 'Modern' Novigrad was developed in the Middle Ages on a tiny islet which was later joined to the mainland. The Venetians arrived as early as the twelth century, and it was later overrun for a time by the Turks. So there is much to see.

Nin is yet another sleepy place with a heyday past. Here, at the edge of a sheltered strip of seawater, and facing the southern end of the island of Pag, this dreamy place sports old Roman columns lying where they fell on the forum. Chickens scratch about on Roman paving stones; an elderly donkey will sometimes avail himself of a piece of carved masonry to discourage a fly worrying his back. Nin cannot have altered much in a thousand years. And, because the level of the Adriatic has gradually risen as the land sinks about 1 m per thousand years — there are considerable remains now submerged in the calm water. The town had, as Roman Aenona, municipal autonomy, but you would never know now that Nin was once such an important centre of ancient Liburnia, later to be the crowning place of the first Croatian king, Tomislav, in AD 924. But this urban centre, recorded by Constantine Porphyrogenitus in the tenth century when it was called Nona, was the bishopric where Bishop Grgur fought for the right to use the Croatian language and the Glagolitic script in the Roman Catholic masses of the time. It is remarkable to think that what he worked for, and won, was not generally adopted by the Catholic Church until the twentieth century. He probably paid a high price, however, as he seems to have disappeared without trace around AD 928.

Close to Nin there is a small village called Petrčane with just one modern and very self-contained hotel with its own shop and hairdressers, etc., beautifully situated at the edge of the sea and backed by huge sweet-scented pinewoods. Walking on the springy pine needles under the trees is something quite special, and so is the heady air. The shore is rocky, but there are flat stone-paved areas for sunbathing, and the sea is warm and clear.

Not far away, Biograd also has a holiday resort at its side. It was once a royal Croatian town built on the remains, probably, of Roman Blandona. Just over a hundred years after Tomislav was crowned in Nin (up the road!), King Peter Krešimir founded a bishopric and built monasteries and churches there. It was at Biograd, too, that Koloman — the Hungarian king — had himself crowned in 1102 with the title *Rex Hungariae, Croatiae et Dalmatiae*. Biograd was even affected by the Crusaders when, in 1202, these stalwart opportunists were bribed by Venice into meanly taking Zadar while on their way to the Middle East. The population of Biograd rose to alarming heights at that time, swollen by the fugitives who came pouring in for shelter when their own town was annexed. Seeing quiet little Biograd now, it is very hard to believe that it had such a virile history though, as always, a little something seems to have rubbed off from the past to show in the inhabitants' faces.

CENTRAL DALMATIA

Within reach of both Zadar and Split airports, and not far south of Biograd, is Šibenik (see Chapter 5) with, a few kilometres outside the town, two very modern holiday resorts. These are Vodice, by a small village, and Solaris. Both are completely self-contained with everything to hand in the way of sports and water sports, and day and evening entertainment. There are holiday clubs, and special amusements for children; but it is well worth exploring outside the resorts for a richer look at scenery and local life.

One of the most interesting excursions goes up river to the Krka Falls, inland from the natural harbour and river mouth at Šibenik. The River Krka gathers its water from the karst (limestone) uplands and — so much clear fresh water is there in Yugoslavia — it never runs short. The Krka River is a curious pale aquamarine colour patched with deep emerald, and very broad in its lower reaches. Edged by hills and deciduous woods, rushes grow in profusion on its banks. To get to the Falls there is now a good road which runs across the uplands with their stony outcrops, short grass and grazing

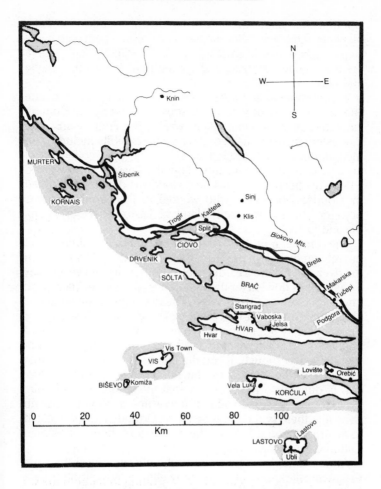

sheep. This country is perfect for sheep farming which is carried on not just for meat and wool but for the production of milk which is made into cheese. As is the case with goats in this type of farming country, the grass is not so rank and lush that it produces milk over-strong in flavour, but rather a milk like a more delicate cow's milk, rich in cream. Here on these uplands it is still possible — as in other rural areas of Yugoslavia — to see shepherds and shepherdesses wandering along with their sheep, and older Grannies spinning wool as they walk.

At the Falls there are now restaurants and open-air cafés. Just up the hill there are some small stone huts through which water, diverted from the top of the Falls runs, powering crude

19

wooden hammers that 'felt' handwoven cloth for hats, blankets and leggings for the national dress. A path with many steps leads below to the foot of the spectacular Falls where there are huge flat rocks and a deep pool in which to bathe and cool off.

It is possible to go further up river by small boat to the little island monastery of Visovac, first established by the Dominicans and later, in 1445, taken over by the Franciscans. The monastery museum has some very rare exhibits including an incunabula of 1490 printed in Venice, a large collection of Turkish documents and, most famous, Aesop's *Fables* dated 1486. This beautifully illustrated work was drawn and printed by Dobriša Dobričević who worked in Dubrovnik and was born on the lovely small island of Lastovo — out to sea beyond Korčula.

The brothers in this island monastery live simply and entirely on their own produce, their diet enriched by fish from the river. The island's garden yields fruits, nuts and vegetables — as well as flowers for their churches — and they have pigs, chickens, even peacocks there. The river surrounding them is about 700 m wide at this point washing round either side of the monastery foundations. To go to this small island of enchantment is like visiting another world — a tiny planet of infinite peace, though, if you dig into its history, you find that there, too, were times of trouble and even temporary exodus.

It is difficult to realise today that this entire area of quiet rural country has had such an interesting history. Further up river still, there is another monastery, Orthodox and dedicated to Sv Arhandjeo (St Michael the Archangel), though in Roman Catholic Croatia.

At one time the region was in the possession of the early Croatian rulers, but later, in the twelfth century, it became a fortified seat of the Knights Templars; a far cry from those Templars who bequeathed their name to London's law centre! In the fourteenth century the knights of the Order of St John took over, and later still in the sixteenth and seventeenth centuries it was — like so much of this part of the Mediterranean basin — bandied to and fro between the Venetians and the Turks. The Venetians always left beautiful buildings behind them, but as a rule the Turks left little beyond a few attractive mosques in those areas of Yugoslavia where they settled. Vrana, a tiny village famous for its huge lake, is an exception. Here the Turks left an irrigation and drainage system, engineered by the Arabian gardeners they brought in to improve the land. Traces of this work can still be seen.

The fortified medieval moated castle at Vrana is now in ruins but — a rare sight in Dalmatia — there are still remains of a Turkish caravanserai which was built in 1644 by a vizier born in Vrana. Another even older relic of the past is the section of a Roman aqueduct built to supply water to Roman Zadar, or Jedera as it was then called.

South of Šibenik is the tiny peninsula of Primošten with, on either side of the village, holiday hotels built on wooded points; plus a sizeable yacht marina. Primošten is famous for its wines — in particular Babić, a red full-bodied wine of delightful flavour. The vineyards can be seen all along the coastal slopes surrounding the peninsula. They face the sun and have that particular gravel soil that produces fine wines both here and in other parts of the country — notably in Hercegovina and in Macedonia.

Primošten has an interesting history. Its people came from inland in the sixteenth century when the Turks chased them out of Bosnia. When they first arrived on the coast, Primošten was an island just off-shore and they built a drawbridge to connect it to the mainland. The people would work the fields and vineyards on the shore during the day and then, at the signal of a tattoo beaten on a drum, would all troop back over the bridge, pulling it up behind them for safety. In fact, the name Primošten comes from the verb *primostiti*, to bridge over.

Gradually the narrow strip of water separating the island from the land began to silt up with the currents, helped by the people in less dangerous times, and a wide causeway now joins Primošten village to the mainland. The people of this little village are very friendly and open-handed. The grape harvest is one of their busiest and happiest times of the year, and if you happen to be there in late September or October, you will see the women with great trays of grapes, often carried on their heads, striding through the village to the presses. A few days later, there will be huge bowls of 'novi Babić' offered around. This delicious new unfinished wine — more like sparkling grape juice — is quite an experience. Never refuse it!

One of the earliest post-war Esperanto conferences was held at Primošten in 1962, organised by some astronomers from Zagreb. A legacy from this early get-together is a series of small garden beds, one for each country, in which each of the delegates left a little something brought from home. There is soil from Japan in one, burnt paper from Hungary in another, and so on.

Nine kilometres south of Primošten, another small village is on what was once an island; this one has a causeway artificially built in the nineteenth century. Rogoznica is an attractive and quiet little place with no massive tourist developments. Very sheltered, and close to the Adriatic Highway, there are pinewoods and superb bays for swimming and sunbathing. Here there is a reminder of Napoleon's short occupation of Dalmatia, which he called the 'Illyrian Provinces' at the beginning of the nineteenth century. At the highest point of the small hill there are remains of a fortification which was begun by the French in 1809. This look-out, no doubt, was used to check that the British fleet — under Admirals Nelson and Fremantle, and Captain William Hoste — was not approaching to disturb the calm!

There are several churches and chapels at Rogoznica including Sv Nikola with its interesting medieval gravestones — or *Stecci* — and a chapel dating from 1324.

A little further south, and nearing Trogir (10 km), and Split, is Marina, one of the most beautiful little hamlets, set at the head of a long slim inlet bordered on one side by profusely flowering oleanders. The shores of the bay are indented with small coves with pebble and coarse-sand beaches.

Marina is quite out of this world. It was first recorded in the thirteenth century and the bishop of Trogir built a castle there in the early sixteenth century: a summer home which could also be used against the Turks when necessary. The gateway with the bishop's coat of arms, a chapel and the keep still survive. There is one small and quite delightful hotel which hangs, crenellated, over the water.

As you progress along this part of the coast towards Split, the area of flat country on the seaward side of the coastal mountains becomes ever more densely cultivated; not just with vineyards, but with peaches, oranges, lemons, nectarines, custard apples and pomegranates — that apple, they say, with which Eve tempted Adam — together with saladings, cucumbers, aubergines and sweet peppers, as well as market flowers.

The entire area is extremely fertile and, though the majority of the produce is sent to Split for distribution, some of it finds its colourful way to the markets of Trogir, that small and perfect gem of medieval architecture and rich history. Trogir's markets sprawl on either side of the main road to Split. On the left is the original covered market with its stone archway, and on the right the huge open-air overflow.

It is only when you get through this overflow that you notice a low bridge spanning a seawater channel to the small islet on which walled and fortified Trogir was built. On the further side of this islet there is a second bridge leading to the much bigger island of Čiovo but, from whichever side you gaze, Trogir — surrounded by water — seems too perfect to be real; a masterpiece of symmetry and beauty. But Trogir is very real, with a strong spirit distilled from early medieval, and even Greek times, and its many treasures draw admirers from all parts of the world.

In spite of its riches, the bustling small community still enjoys a busy urban life. Its holiday hotels are a kilometre or two up the road, set on a completely protected stretch of shore where you can find up-to-date self-contained apartments to hire in a 'village' as well as the main modern hotel. Close to the new buildings there is a series of open-air and covered restaurants near the sea, with terraces and gardens, where national dishes cooked on charcoal and fish grilled fresh from the sea fill the air with that special aroma that drives the taste-buds mad. Once smelled, this mixture of olive oil, rosemary and bay leaves, together with the scent of sun-drenched pine trees and grilling food, forever spells Dalmatia.

Old Trogir itself is famous architecturally for many things. First, there are the walls and defence towers behind which King Bela IVth and his court tricked the Mongolian hordes from Central Asia in 1242. Surrounding the tiny water-locked city during the night, these ferocious pillagers from Central Asia called out across the narrow waterway their terms of surrender, only to be met by a stony silence on the king's orders. To the astonishment of everyone inside the walls, by the next morning the attackers had vanished. It seemed like a miracle but in fact they had received news that their Khan, Ogadai — son of Genghis Khan — had died and they were hot-footing it back to Bukhara and Samarkand doubtless to take part in the squabbling over who the next ruler would be!

This incident seems to typify Trogir's serendipity. It is a happy place with a charm difficult to define. Perhaps it is helped by its greatest treasure, the incomparable bas-relief of the Greek god Kairos, honey-coloured and forever beautiful. Kairos is housed in a small museum attached to the convent of Benedictine nuns and their church of Sv Nikola. Founded in 1064, this convent is one of the earliest in Dalmatia. Until recently, to see this carving of the god of the propitious and fleeting moment entailed knocking at the door of the 'closed' order of nuns and waiting for a key to appear on the shelf of a revolving cupboard. But 'progress' has intruded even here, and now the nuns appear among the treasures of the museum and church, which also include a valuable Gothic polyptych and other early paintings, as well as a painted Gothic crucifix.

Kairos, it is thought, is a first century BC copy of an original Greek third century BC relief. It was lost for hundreds of years, and only rediscovered in 1928. The young god's hair seems gently wind-blown; he holds scales in his outstretched arms; and his face in profile, with its straight Greek nose, is eager yet hesitant, supplicating and uncertain, as if even he cannot believe that the perfect fleeting moment has come.

The main square in Trogir is very large with some beautiful Venetian houses (one now a museum), the fifteen-century City Loggia with its bas-relief of Justice (about 1471) where the business of running the city was conducted, and the clock tower, once part of the chapel of St Seb'astian. But the biggest building in the square is the cathedral (13th to 15th centuries) of both Romanesque and Gothic architecture. On the exterior, it is the huge carved stone portal of Radovan, created by this master of stone-masonry and carving in 1240, that almost overwhelms one. The carved figures are so delicate and intricate, and show all the scenes of life and of nature on their deeply cut stone pilasters. Trogir is justly proud of its history and its treasures and, though so close to Split (28 km), is a complete small entity with an independent life of its own.

Outside its 'sea-gates', at the furthest point from the main road, there is an exquisite second loggia (dated 1527) which is now used as a fish market. Buying fish — perhaps fresh steaks of tunny straight from the sea — is a delightful, though incongruous, experience in such a setting; only matched by watching a film in the grounds of the huge fifteenth-century castle nearby, or sitting in the delicious little 'glorietta' or folly which Napoleon's general, Marmont, left behind as a monument after his occupation of Trogir during the Napoleonic era.

Trogir lies at one side of the long Bay of Castles — the Kaštelanski Zaljev — with Split and Roman Salona at the other end of the bay. Here, on the coastal plain, is Split airport, with the mountains on its northern side. The bay is very sheltered and there are seven medieval villages with the remains of keeps, built for safety, in each. It is these fortified towers (originally there were 13) which have given the bay its name. As well as fruit trees, there are large pine woods in this area and several modern hotels have been built among the trees. The swimming and bathing are good and so is the bus service between Trogir and Split; the air is particularly soft and balmy, and protocol is at a minimum. But the eastern end of the bay, including the historical site of Roman Salona, is becoming very industrialised with factories, a big cement works, and new housing between the sea and the coastal mountains.

In the mountains, and visible from Split (see Chapter 5), is a castle perched on a col. This huge fortress is Klis Castle, 360 m above sea level, yet only 8 km away from the port of Split. Looking up at this eyrie is awe-inspiring; looking down from its heights in either direction is terrifying!

There is a small hamlet clustered round the base of the pinnacle on which the castle is built and this village was, in the Middle Ages, the administrative centre of the surrounding plains. Even earlier, the rich Romans living at sea level in Salona had moved up the slopes to build their country villas, the palatial Roman idea of a weekend cottage. The earliest Croatian records of Klis, now small and peaceful, date from AD 852, the time when Croatia, and with it Dalmatia, was ruled by princes, or Bans, about 70 years before Tomislav, the first king, was crowned at Nin. In the later Middle Ages the area passed into the hands of the rich Šubić family and, in 1242, that same King Bela IVth (whose luck later held when he was beleaguered in Trogir) took refuge in Klis from the Tartar hordes, later landing up inside the walls of Split where he was not over-welcome. Leaving his wife and his small daughters

Klis, fortified against the Turkish invaders in the fifteenth century

behind — one child died of a virus and her sarcophagus still rests over the mausoleum doorway — Bela then repaired to Trogir.

Klis was fortified in the fifteenth century when the Ottoman Empire began to encroach on the territory behind the coastal mountains, but the Turks didn't actually take Klis until 1537 after a siege that lasted for months. During that siege help for the defenders came from many parts of the coast — even from far-off Senj — and one of Senj's most famous pirate-patriots, Captain Petar Krušić, lost his life there.

Once the garrison had been finally overcome, the Turkish invaders were able to control the whole of inland Dalmatia. This situation obtained for more than 100 years until the Venetians, well-established along the coast, finally managed to take the Klis fortress in 1648. During the Turkish occupation the stronghold was enlarged and altered with three rings of defence walls. They built a mosque within the walls — the body of which was turned into a church in later years and the minaret destroyed. The fortress has impressive arched gate-ways into the interior and there is a terrific atmosphere to the place. No wonder it has been used for various film locations during the last few years.

The view down from the fortress is vertiginous, and cars on the roads below look more like ants than machines. The road inland carries on to another small town, Sinj, also on a steep hill above a surrounding plain. Sinj too, had its heroic battles with the Turks. The way to this second citadel runs through land splattered with white rocks with, in between, tiny circumscribed fields of rich red earth, intensely cultivated, though sometimes only a few metres in diameter.

Sinj is famous for its day of jousting on horseback in ancient costume each year. Known as Sinjska Alka, this most exciting of festivals takes place on a Sunday in August in commemmoration of the battle in 1715 when the attacking Turks were vanquished, though in a majority of three to one. The young men of Sinj train throughout the year on some beautiful horses specially kept for the event. The sport is for the riders to career down the steep tree-lined road in the town with a lance. They must spear the ring — or *Alka* — suspended above their heads from the trees. The man who, on horseback, spears the middle and smallest ring within the *Alka* the most times in three tries, is fêted with the band playing and drums rolling. It is a terrific festival held for the local population. But visitors are always welcome and there is now a modern hotel in Sinj to accommodate them.

After Split, the road continues down the coast passing small villages with names like Mali Rat and Veli Rat (Rat means nothing more sinister than 'point' or 'cape') where elderly black-clad ladies in summer sit at stalls by the wayside, selling peaches, grapes and soft drinks. Drinking alcohol while driving is highly hazardous in Yugoslavia and liable to gather large penalties, particularly for the locals, who lose their licences more easily than falling off a log.

A little further on from the Rats (28 km from Split), the road enters the town and port of Omiš where, at a right-angled bend in the road, the River Cetina enters the sea, and the unusual shaped Omiš fishing boats can be seen in the port. These ships are a speciality of Omiš and look from the bows a bit like basking walruses.

As with so many of these small ports and coastal villages, Omiš was inhabited in the days of Rome. From the twelfth to the fifteenth centuries it was ruled by Croatian princes of the Kačić and, later, Šubić families but fell inevitably to the power of Venice in 1444. There are remains of a fortress, city walls, and gates; some notable pictures by old Italian masters such as Palma the Younger and Matteus Ingoli; and, on the right bank of the Cetina river, a pre-Romanesque chapel of Sv Petar with a cupola and frieze mentioned in tenth-century documents.

Inland from Omiš, the River Cetina flows through a beautifully wooded gorge from its source near Sinj, having doubled back through the Dinaric Mountains. There is a good road along the river from Omiš and it is a very worthwhile journey either by car, or on one of the organised excursions from the Makarska Riviera. At the head of the gorge is a hydro-electric power station and, a little further up, some old and very picturesque water mills — the *Radmanove Mlinice* — whose buildings now provide restaurants and open-air terraces under beautiful and very large trees. Along a path upstream from the mills you come to some spectacular waterfalls.

Omiš, though chiefly a fishing port and small administrative centre, has bowed to tourism enough to build a summer hotel and provide a camping site.

Beyond Omiš, Donja Brela marks the beginning of the Makarska Riviera, a favoured stretch of sheltered coast with the five small ports of Donja Brela, Baška Voda, Makarska, Tučepi and Podgora; all of which have very good, rather large, modern hotels close to the sheltered long beaches, with a quiet sea road connecting them along the 15 km of the Riviera. The main highway runs behind the ports at the foot of the Biokovo mountains.

Although the hotels here — some open in winter and very popular with older people — are new and provide many facilities like tennis courts, water-sports, shops, and music, the area above the shore on the steep slopes of Biokovo is very old. Life, before tourism, must have been hard on the stark slopes. There are roads up to stone-built, often stone-roofed villages, and over the mountains. These roads, well engineered, hairpin their way skywards with craggy bluffs on the one hand, sheer drops on the other, until they reach the upland pastures of the plains beyond.

The villages on the slopes live a separate life from the sybaritic existence near the sea, fhough many of the young men and women who work in the hotels come down from their homes on the hills each day. After a stiff walk up to one of these hamlets — which seem, sometimes, to cling by their eyebrows to the mountain slopes — there is always a glass of wine or *rakija* (a Dalmatian *eau-de-vie*) to be found in a tiny café.

From Donja Brela there is now an excellent road across the Biokovo chain to Imotski, the wine-processing centre of the area. The factory, apart from producing its own-brand wines, also bottles wines under several other labels. For instance, you can find an Imotski Vranac, but these wines should not be confused with the white and yellow labelled Vranac — a particularly fine red wine produced only from the original vineyards in Montenegro.

Imotski has two other claims to fame: the Red and the Blue lakes, deep down in the folds of the mountains outside the town. Their presence and their brilliant colours are hard to explain. Some people think they are the result of a huge meteorite striking the karst rock at some prehistoric time.

The Biokovo range is rich in alpine flowers, small wild animals and caves for pot-holers. And there are some superb crags for serious climbers.

The main centre at sea level is Makarska, the small fishing port with its almost enclosed natural harbour. It was one of the first places in Central Dalmatia to be developed for international tourism after the last war, and the first hotel on its riviera was Hotel Jadran at Tučepi. A little old-fashioned compared with its younger counterparts, it still has a certain charm that perhaps the others, with their modern efficiency, as yet lack. Local life still hinges on the fishing harbours but there are now hotels strung all along this stretch of coast. Its protected shores, the small coastal road under the shade of trees — more a quiet promenade than a road for vehicles — and the pine trees actually growing on the beaches, make

28

Makarska and its Riviera very attractive. And, because there is so much room to spare along the 15 km of its coastline, there are big gardens and parks, small private houses, cafés and restaurants near the sea, plus a very beautiful old court or manor house near Tučepi which has recently been converted into a small hotel. Thanks to its position, with the Biokovo range to its north and the islands of Brač and Hvar offshore to the south, the Riviera is particularly sheltered and gets an average of about 2,000 hours of sunshine a year.

It is in Makarska that the small shell museum can be found. It has been arranged in the crypt of the fifteenth-century Franciscan monastery by Dr Fra. Jure Radić. The exhibits have come from all over the world and are really fascinating. The nuns make and sell shell and coral jewellery to help cover expenses.

The most easterly resort in the area is Podgora — literally 'Below the mountain heights' — where the Biokovo mountains come down very close to the sea. There is a spectacular war memorial above the port to Tito's Partisans. This huge memorial, carved in stark white stone, is in the form of a stylised gull, one wing broken, descending to earth. It represents the Partisans' flight to the islands from the mainland in 1943, and their coming again to the coast with the newly-formed Partisan navy as the occupation began to recede, pushed back by Tito's forces, and helped by the Allies (on my last visit I saw a wreath for 43 British Commando).

The Yugoslavs have built magnificent memorials throughout the country — most of them very poignant and particularly apt for the individual events which led to their creation. Locally there is sometimes a ceremony of remembrance for lost sons and daughters. I was present on one such occasion at Podgora. The words were spoken as from the voice of a mother who had lost her sons. I found myself as moved as the Dalmatian men and women around me, who stood quietly weeping, not just in sadness but in gratitude for the freedom that the great sacrifice had given to them and to their country. In that most difficult time, the 1st and 2nd Dalmatinska Brigada lost almost all their men in a blocking stand at Sutjeska in Bosnia, thus allowing the majority of the Partisans to escape the pincer movement of the enemy through a narrow gorge. It was here in the Sutjeska area that a British officer, Captain Bill Stuart, was killed. With Captain William Deakin he was parachuted in to the Partisans in the early summer of 1943 and caught up in this action. Here, too, Tito was wounded, but lived to form a new Socialist Republic of Yugoslavia after the war, thanks in part to that heroic stand.

The memorial to this battle, deep in the woods of Bosnia, is yet another overwhelmingly moving place to visit.

SOUTHERN DALMATIA

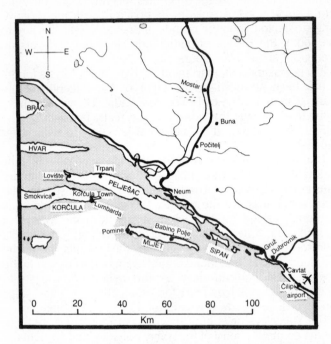

Not far along the coast from Makarska, the mountains of the island of Korčula can be seen dimly over the extremity of the equally hilly Pelješac Peninsula which stretches parallel to the mainland for 80 km. Inside the long arm of the peninsula, the mainland breaks dramatically at the delta of the Neretva River.

This river has a special, almost sentimental, significance for many South Slavs, and in particular Dalmatians, whose early forefathers came along this waterway in the seventh century, migrating from behind the Carpathians in Central Europe. Those Slav tribes made their way along the Neretva in their search for a better and more peaceful life. Their ancestors had accompanied the war-like Avar tribes to the region a hundred years earlier. This time they came in peace to settle permanently in these superbly fertile lands by the river and beyond.

Century after century the waters of the Neretva have cut ever more deeply into the rock of the wooded hills through which they flow; a drive up this river to the highlands from which it begins is a memorable journey. It is a fascinating thought that the way carved out by the river which led the Slavs south, was the path through which the early Greeks journeyed north, about a thousand years earlier, to get to the rich silver deposits of Bosnia. There are many proofs of those Greek incursions into Bosnia where a number of Corinthian pottery vessels have been found.

At one side of the Neretva delta there is the large commercial port of Kardeljevo. This was formerly known as Ploče but, after a local referendum, the name was changed as a mark of respect for one of Tito's most forward-thinking friends and ministers.

Kardeljevo is sultry and very well protected — both climatically and strategically — but there is a car ferry which runs several times a day from the port to the Pelješac Peninsula, shortening the road to Korčula island considerably, though not the time of the journey.

Scenically much more beautiful, is a journey up the river to Mostar, passing such delights as Buna and Počitelj on the way. It is not surprising that the tourist agencies organise many coach excursions in summer to savour such attractions. There is a good road that runs beside the river to Mostar and far beyond. Through awe-inspiring gorges and mountain peaks, tunnels and ravines, it leads even as far as the Zagreb/Belgrade auto route — taking in either the Jajce Falls and Banja Luka, or Sarajevo on the way. After leaving the sea at Kardeljevo, the road traverses the Neretva delta, then settles down at river level. A few kilometres on, there is a right-hand turn along the River Buna. This side road is well worth exploring. It ends at a sheer vertical mountain rock from which the river water pours through a rounded hole. A very old Turkish house stands beside the outlet and, as the river flattens out, there is a trout farm, a very small fishing hotel, an open-air restaurant and abundant fish, with a water wheel that turns the spit roaster over charcoal when lamb is in season.

Along the main road towards Mostar there is another remarkable sight. This is the complete fortified Turkish village of Počitelj which rears up to the right of the road in a series of ancient buildings clinging to the slopes. There is a Han, baths, many houses, a mosque (dating from 1592) near the top and, crowning everything, a fortress from pre-Turkish times which was strengthened in 1444. This remarkable relic of medieval and Ottoman life in Bosnia/Hercegovina was for a long time in ruins, but an enlightened local authority has restored it and its excellent Han (where only Turkish food is served), and the mosque. Some of the houses, also modernised, are used as an artists' colony and a small tourist shop has particularly attractive pictures, plates, textiles, etc.

There are many cherry trees in the area and, in the first week of June, they hold a 'Cherry Week' — *Trešnja Sedmica* — with cherries and their stalks plaited into fantastic 'ropes' and other shapes.

From Počitelj it is not far to the outskirts of Mostar itself. The main, rather ugly, stretch of road skirting the town tells nothing of the oriental flavour of the old part. But, on foot, meandering through the winding streets towards the ancient and famous bridge is like entering an eastern world, in spite of the many visitors who naturally gather there.

The road down to the marble structure which spans the aquamarine and very deep water, is cobbled and has Turkish houses, cafés and craft workshops along the way. Mostar was always a centre for silver, copper and leather work and the souvenirs — made on the spot — are attractive, often useful, and not expensive.

The bridge, gleaming white, arches over the river with a span of 30 m and a height of 24 m. It is slim, its arch steep, and has a guard tower on each bank. The building of this lovely bridge took ten years in the fifteenth century and was constructed by Hajrudin, a well-known Turkish architect and pupil of the builder of the Blue Mosque in Istanbul. It is said that his first structure fell down into the river just as it was finished, and the Turkish Bey threatened instant death if he didn't succeed at the second attempt. The mortar between the marble slabs was mixed with white-of-egg and milk. He succeeded so well that the bridge — many pedestrians crossing it each day — still stands to delight the eye with its sheer simple beauty and symmetry. Its picture adorns one of Mostar's best-known white wines, *Žilavka*.

The grape from which *Žilavka* is made grows only in Hercegovina and has been cultivated round Mostar since the Romans were there. The happy combination of this particular grape, plus the climate and the special gravel soil of the area, give the wine a unique flavour which is neither sweet nor acid. Mentioned by the king of Bosnia (Stjepan Tvrtko) as early as 1353, it became, several centuries later, a favourite wine of the Hapsburgs and, in the nineteenth century, the main vineyard of Čitluk produced wine exclusively for the royal court in Vienna. Needless to say, Čitluk has won many golden seals of approval in all parts of Europe — including Victorian London in 1898.

The bridge in Mostar stands, too, as a symbol of fearlessness for Mostar's young men. It is a tradition that they jump

The famous Turkish bridge in Mostar's oriental quarter

from the apex of the bridge into the deep waters below. Some of them will even jump for tourist cameras to record — at a small price.

There are several mosques in the town, some still working, as well as an open-air market for fruit, vegetables and spices. The churches include both Catholic and Orthodox at this meeting place of religions, and there are a few Bogomil graves scattered about, too. Mostar has several hotels, one of them very new and modern on the farther side of the Neretva, near an even older bridge whose foundations are Roman.

A visit to Mostar would be sad if it didn't include a meal of oriental-Bosnian dishes served in a Han: perhaps *čorba*, a thick meat and vegetable soup to start with; then Kebabs (*ražnjići*), or maybe a 'Bosnian Pot', or peppers, onions and tomatoes stuffed with meat and rice and served in a spicy sauce. Sweet cakes such as *baklava*, or *tufahije* — apples stuffed with walnuts and butter and cooked in syrup — can all be washed down with *Žilavka*, and finished off with Turkish coffee and Turkish delight. They do it all well in Mostar!

Bosnia/Hercegovina, although an inland republic, does have a small section of the coast. Its only resort is Neum with one rather functional hotel and a number of private seaside homes. Sheltered not only by Pelješac, but also by a smaller peninsula called Klek, Neum has its own claim to fame. The republic of medieval Dubrovnik, in order to discomfit its arch rival Venice, granted the Turks who ruled over Bosnia in the seventeenth century something the Ottoman overlords had always wanted: an outlet to the sea. So, between Neum and Klek, a tiny portion of the Dalmatian coast — only about 11 km long — still belongs to Bosnia. There are frequent wry jokes about this fact. All the same, many Bosnians take the outlet seriously ·enough to build their *weekendicas* here, rather than elsewhere. On the Klek Peninsula itself, there are the ruins of a castle and many fourteenth- and fifteenth-century tombstones.

From Neum to the huge fortified walls of Ston and Mali (or Little) Ston, where the Pelješac Peninsula joins the mainland, is only about 18 km. At first sight it is hard to take in the fact of these massive defences — not just surrounding Ston, but climbing up and right over the steep maquis-clad hill and down the other side — with guard towers and walls wide enough to walk on. But Ston and Mali Ston, in the Middle Ages, were an 'outpost of empire' to the Republic of Dubrovnik. At the very top of the hill separating the two villages Dubrovnik manned a semaphore which signalled to the old city some 40 km to the south-east.

Ston has one hotel, recently renovated and useful for one-night stays, or more. It has kept its 'B' category designation and now earns it, though it was a local joke before! But who cares, when at Mali Ston they produce some of the best oysters it is possible to obtain, as well as fat mussels, and *prstaci*, the delicious razor-shell bi-valves. Since the early Middle Ages Ston has been a centre for the produce of sea salt. The old salt-pans are still worked, and the store-houses for this product — beautifully built of stone and looking more like cupolaed churches than warehouses — are still in use.

Ston, in former times, was responsible for all the salt needed in a huge area. Each of the many salt drying-pans was named after a saint, and the Sv Nikola pan was kept for the people of Ston to use without payment. The sea water for the pans arrives along a narrow channel, straight from the open and very saline Adriatic.

Inside the walls of the little village there are many very beautiful carved stone buildings of former times. Quiet streets climb the hill, their stone balconies adorned with old oil cans used as flower-pots for geraniums, jasmine and bright oleanders. Life goes on peaceably — still centred under a huge tree in the stone-paved square — next to the local café-restaurant and the hotel.

Mali Ston — on the other side of the steep hill but only a few hundred metres round the base by road — is even quieter with a big harbour for small boats, many old tall houses that seem to be sleeping, and a restaurant hanging over the water outside the vast defence walls. This restaurant is a side-line of the people who produce the oysters — in a big way — flying them out to all parts of the country, as well as selling them, and the mussels, locally. These shell-fish are best produced not just in pure salt water, but with a mixture of fresh water and salt; and the oyster beds are in a shallow bay where fresh water springs emerge in winter from under the sea.

The next big bay along the coast is called Slano and here, on the edge of the small fishing port, is a most attractively built hotel. Low, and with stone walls and red roofs, Hotel Admiral blends with the village scene. There are flower-beds of pink and white oleanders, pebble beaches, local cafés and restaurants — for holidays an idyllic kind of life. On one arm of the inlet — about 2 km away — there is an altogether different kind of hotel, equally modern but shaped in egg-box style. This now caters solely for nudists. The local people, as well as growing grapes, vegetables and olives, also collect herbs for medicine from the surrounding hills, such as sage, bay, thymes and wormwood.

Slano means 'salty'. There are always stories attached to odd names and this one comes, they say, from the time when a medieval Bosnian princess saw the blue sea for the first time. She was entranced, rushing in to bathe, and to drink the water — imagining it to be a great lake. 'Oh Slano!' she is supposed to have said. And Slano it has remained!

Only 29 km from Dubrovnik, with a frequent bus service, is Trsteno. Trsteno has no large holiday facilities but is well worth visiting for anyone interested in trees. In the small square where the bus stops are two remarkable and huge plane trees. Each is more than 400 years old and the girth of the larger one's trunk is 11 m. They are unique in this part of Europe. Then, towards the sea, is the former palace of a Dubrovnik patrician family with, in the gardens, an arboretum containing many different species of trees and flowering shrubs, including an example of that pre-evolutionary 'false' tree, the Gingko, with its fern-like leaves.

There is one more long inlet before the outskirts of Dubrovnik and its international port of Gruž come into view. This is Zaton, with two very attractive fishing hamlets — Big and Little Zaton — with old stone houses and good quays. They are not to be confused with that other Zaton near Šibenik. So far, Big and Little Zaton have, except for a small camping site on the shore, been left very much as they were, though nearby at Orašac there are now extensive developments for tourism in the form of a modern self-contained holiday village.

South-east of Dubrovnik (see Chapter 5) there are several small satellite resorts that combine a relaxed seaside life with the possibility of popping into Dubrovnik when one wishes. The first of these resorts, which are all clustered round the wide Bay of Župa, is Kupari — actually named after an old brickyard. This was a thriving resort even before the last war when the hotel was managed by a Swiss national. That situation would not be tolerated these days when all hotel staff are Yugoslav, though it will be interesting to see how the new laws on foreign investment and holiday time-sharing will work out in this respect.

Close to Kupari, on an inner curve of the bay and backed by

Orlando's statue in Dubrovnik; his arm was used as measuring stick in the Middle Ages

a large camping and caravan site, is Srebreno with just one hotel, Orlando. The name comes from a Dubrovnikan knight whose statue is near the clock-tower in Stradun, the main street. Srebreno is a happy place, and the hotel is surrounded by trees under which you can dance. You can drink and eat barbecued food at the cafés, and almost roll into the calm sea.

Next along the bay is Mlini, which takes its name from an old water-mill. There is fresh water running to the sea from the mountains just behind and the mill-house is now a café and restaurant with a modern hotel built near at hand. The highway runs at the back of all these resorts leaving them free of all but local traffic. Mlini is a winter as well as a summer resort, and popular with older, longer-staying visitors for an off-season holiday.

Before reaching Cavtat at the further end of the Župa Bay, there is another modern hotel complex literally built on to the steep slope of shrub-covered ground that rises from the sea. This complex, called Plat, is a large post-war development with one hotel, reached down paths and steps, close to the sea, and the second, under the same management, perched above near the Magistrala Highway, and called Ambasador.

Cavtat, founded by the Illyrians, is anything but new, though there are many post-war hotels clustered round its wide, well protected part of the bay. The newest of these, Hotel Croatia, is considered one of the finest luxury hotels in the country with a huge conference hall, an 'English Club Room', several restaurants, and a superb position on the outer arm of the wooded bay.

In ancient Greek times Cavtat was called Epidaurus — later to become Roman Epidaurum. Some people think there are the remains of Greek foundations under the sea in the bay, but this has never been proved. What are clear to see, in the gardens of Hotel Croatia, are Roman sarcophagi and other stones.

The town, as a bishopric, was first recorded in AD 530. But a hundred years later the Avars, on their rampage south from the Carpathians, destroyed the city and the population fled to safer homes; some of them moving to the small islet on which Dubrovnik was originally founded. Cavtat's old houses and streets are curiously peaceful and the population, while hospitably welcoming its summer influx of visitors, never loses its identity, filling the old houses with members of its own families in summer, as well as visitors. The people of Cavtat are proud of their heritage and their past; proud of their national dress; and proud to point out the grand mausoleum built by one of their rich sons who, though his family had waxed rich in South America, still preferred to come 'home' to Cavtat for his final rest.

The airport of Dubrovnik, which takes its name from the village of Čilipi is very close to Cavtat. The coast, after the Bay of Župa, becomes hostile with sheer cliffs up from the sea, but these cliffs slope gently inland towards the narrow valley in

National costumes are still seen, especially for folklore when the old single stringed gusle is also in evidence

which the airport lies. Čilipi airport is one of the most attractive at which to land. There is nearly always a welcoming blast of warm air to greet you as you leave the plane in summer and, just outside the buildings, a beautifully land-scaped cactus garden has been cultivated where coaches and taxis wait.

The village of Čilipi is set at the edge of the long valley of Konavli. It has a huge church, and in the square in front there are performances of folklore each Sunday morning. The costumes are particularly beautiful in this region, with embroidery on aprons and bodices and red gold-trimmed pill-box hats. The Konavli valley is a rich agricultural area and many of the women don national dress to go with their produce to the market within the walls of Dubrovnik on weekday mornings. It is a brave sight.

Towards the further end of the valley there is a sign on the main road saying 'Konovoski Dvoru' — Konavli Court. If you follow this side road you come to one of the nicest 'country' restaurants imaginable where they bake fresh bread in the old ovens, put the best local wine on the tables, spit-roast a variety of meats, and serve some excellent Dalmatian dishes. The 'Court' is at the source of the Ljuta River, so in hot weather you eat under trees, to the music of the water-mill that still churns its way round at one side: altogether time out from the cares of life!

There is an inland town about 25 km along a good road which crosses the coastal mountain chain to the north of the Konavli valley. This town is Trebinje. Although an industrial centre, it is worth visiting for the buildings left over from Turkish occupation. But, continuing along the coast road for only a few kilometres more, the old Croatia/Montenegro frontier is at hand with the entire Montenegrin Littoral ahead.

THE MOUNTAINS AND LITTORAL OF MONTENEGRO

Although crossing the old frontier between Croatia and Montenegro goes unnoticed these days, it does very soon become apparent that Montenegro is, and always has been, a different country. Its name gives the key. Black Mountain — in Serbo-Croat *Crna Gora* — is not just one peak but a whole chunk of the earth's surface thrown up into great crags that surround high small plateaux and pastures in the interior. Until this century Montenegro had almost no outlet to the sea and, although this mountain-girt region made life extremely difficult to support, the very fact of its inaccessibility and barren stony land was a major factor in its safety. Montenegro was, though encircled by Turkish forces for hundreds of years, never completely occupied, managing to keep both its integrity and much of its land.

The coast, until the nineteenth century, belonged by and large to Dalmatia. That coastline, I think, surpasses even the rest of Yugoslavia's attractive shores for sheer beauty. Certainly it is the most dramatic, its high mountains swooping down almost to the sea itself. The bays sweep southwards in a series of wide curves, each of them enclosed by attractive rocks. Between Budva and Petrovac the stark white of karst rock gives way to a deep pink the colour of red marble, heightening the effect of hills and beaches even more. The

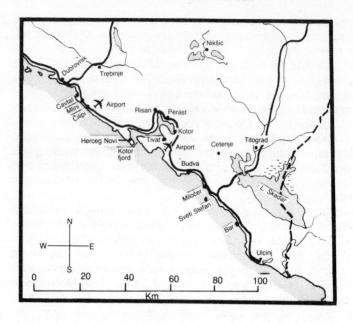

beaches are made of very fine stone — resembling the coarse
sands of Cornwall — though in Montenegro they are rose pink
rather than yellow. The slopes are thickly planted with olive
trees. Nikola (1860–1918), Montenegro's only king, would
only issue a marriage licence after the prospective bridegroom
had planted the required number of olives. The cost of
Nikola's marriage licences, so beneficial to his country, is still
apparent today. Mimosas and pomegranates grow in all
sheltered areas, too. And this most southerly section of the
Yugoslav coast is perceptibly warmer than it is farther north.

There are now many coastal resorts in Montenegro, and the
first you come to by road are those on the shores of the deep
mountain-lined fjord of Kotor. The fjord, from its entrance at
Herceg Novi to its innermost town, Kotor, is more than 14
nautical miles, going directly by ship; and to go round the
entire inlet by road is a journey of about 95 km. The shores
were first peopled by Illyrian tribes who set up, in about 250
BC, an independent State along the entire fjord coast. The
ancient Greeks also discovered this splendid inlet as early as
the 4th century BC, on their way up the Adriatic to the islands
of Korčula, Hvar, Vis and, further north, Cres. Later, in the
wars of 229–168 BC, the Romans gradually subjugated the
area, destroying the Illyrian state of Queen Teuta at her
capital, Risan, and generally occupying and Romanising the

40

fjord. This state of affairs lasted until the fall of the Western Empire in AD 476 when the Ostrogoths arrived to take control for a time; later still, in the sixth century it came under Byzantine rule. All the main settlements of those ancient times have survived, together with some outstanding archaeological and historical remains.

The fjord is very warm in summer, though the sea is about 45 m deep in the middle. Herceg Novi, with its smaller sister Igalo, faces the open sea from its position in the outer bay. It has a huge harbour suitable for large international shipping, and the oldest part of the town is set in tiers above the harbour. Defence walls guard the original citadel which includes a 'Bloody Tower'. A fifteenth-century clock-tower over a gateway marks the entrance to the oriental part of the city where you find steep cobbled streets of houses.

Sadly, the earthquake of 1979, which affected so much of Montenegro, left its toll in Herceg Novi. But there has been massive and intensive rebuilding with anti-tremor measures featuring in all the large blocks of flats, public buildings and hotels. Holiday hotels are, of course, near the sea at both Herceg Novi and Igalo where there is a huge clinic for rheumatic diseases. It was here that President Tito had treatment in his last years.

On a wooded slope near the old town there is a monastery well worth seeing. Set among woods of cypress, oak and laurels, Savina monastery has not one but two churches as well as cloistered living quarters for the monks. And there is a rich treasury and library. The 'new' church, built in 1777–9, was constructed by Nikola Foretić of the island of Korčula. Korčula's stone-masons and the local white stone have both been in demand far from their native island.

On a hill above Kotor fjord there is an interesting chapel which contains the graves of a number of the Knights of St John of Malta. They lost their lives taking part in the Venetian action which finally broke the Turkish occupation of Herceg Novi in 1687.

For anyone wishing to cross the fjord on their way south without driving all the way round, there is a non-stop car and coach ferry between the villages of Kamenari and Lepetane on the further side. Lepetane has some particularly beautiful stone houses. These dwellings were used — so the story goes — by the sea captains of Kotor temporarily to install their ship-board girl-friends ashore. They then went dutifully home to their wives and families who lived in the towns of Morinj, Risan, Perast and Kotor out of sight of Lepetane. It is also said that chains were sometimes stretched across from one side to the other of the straits just under the surface to discourage pirate ships from entering the inner bays.

Morinj is still a sleepy village, with nothing much more than warm sea and a few cafés and houses. But Risan has recently built itself a modern hotel on the shore — the Teuta — and has an attractive small beach. The star attraction at Risan is the remarkably well-preserved Roman mosaic floor of a *villa rustica* depicting, in fine coloured mosaics, a striking portrait of the god Hypnos.

Just before Perast there are two tiny islets just off-shore: Sv Djordje – St George — and Gospa od Škrpjela — Our Lady of the Stones. Sv Djordje is very small and barely big enough to hold the ancient Benedictine monastery and the church, first mentioned in 1166.

Gospa od Škrpjela began life as a small rocky outcrop barely holding its head above water. It is within about 100 m of Sv Djordje and less than 800 m from Perast. Two stories are marked in its personal calendar each year, though the actual days are liable to fluctuate according to expediency. The first legend concerns the island's inception as a religious foundation. The story goes that a sailor was wrecked near the outcrop of the rock in a storm. He clung to the rock and vowed to build a church to the Virgin if he survived. But the rock needed enlarging, and so all the seagoing men of the fjord started to off-load stones as they passed by in their boats; thus the island was gradually formed. Construction of the church began in 1630, and the beautiful copper cupola which stands out a bright turquoise blue was added in 1725. The interior is richly decorated, the walls and ceilings covered in paintings of religious scenes, and where there is room about 2,500 votive silver plaques showing scenes of Perast's seafaring life have been hung. On the altar is a painting of the Madonna by Lovro Dobričević, a fifteenth-century painter. This picture has always been credited with miraculous powers, and one story concerns the year 1654 when, on 28 August, a would-be invasion by the Turks scattered in disarray when the Virgin appeared to them in horror-striking guise, saving the community of Kotor. The Virgin of the Stones is processed each year by boat to the church of Sv Nikola, the parish church of Perast, later returning to the island. In one of the boats in the procession the men are armed, in memory of the Turkish threat.

Perast, the next small village and harbour, doesn't seem big enough in this century to have had such a grand past. But not only did several rich patrician families contribute by building their houses and palazzos there, but it was the home of a very famous naval college which, at one time, rivalled the equally well-known nautical school at Kotor. So highly thought of was Perast as a training centre for young officers, that Peter the Great of Russia sent his naval officer-cadets there. Today the museum, which is housed in one of the palazzos, is ample evidence of just how well-known the Perast naval college became.

The road by the sea is very narrow and, in the last few years, with the advent of the ubiquitous caravan, there have been some glorious traffic jams; but all this has now been disposed of with the building of a small by-pass around the old village, and behind the very attractive stone mansion which has been turned into an hotel.

At the innermost end of the fjord the town of Kotor is on Unesco's World Heritage list and, in spite of wars, earthquakes, pirates, and other calamities, is still a very remarkable and equally ancient centre of civilisation. The city walls and fortresses which climb up to the top of the hill of St John are 4.8 km long, up to 20 m high in some parts, and 15 m in width. They have been built and rebuilt over an entire millennium. There are four city gates (one with three tiers of portals) into the old city, and happily these outer defences withstood the last strong earth tremors of 1979 with only minor damage, though the old houses and churches within the walls suffered a great deal.

With international as well as Yugoslav aid, the authorities in Montenegro are determined that their old cities and religious buildings shall be rebuilt for posterity, following the original plans and façades, though the cost of such an operation is extremely high. They realise that, without the wealth passed down to them by history, tourism has little or nothing to 'feed' on and Kotor, Budva and Ulcinj are now rising again from the devastation. These great earthquakes, travelling along their previous routes, have hit the area — including Dubrovnik — in every third century since records were kept. The one before 1979 was in 1667, when the tremors caused such terrible damage to Dubrovnik. Dubrovnik was built again on exactly the same plan as before. In Kotor, too, the original city plan and façades will be adhered to in the rebuilding.

Only three days after the last earthquake I walked through the broken streets and squares of Kotor, which were guarded by the police. And I smelt the sad smell of death in the old city; though there were few human casualties, the very heart of the town seemed dead. In 1986 I walked there again, among rushing cement carriers and huge meshes of iron. I went into Sv Trifun's cathedral (a second great edifice replacing the original ninth-century circular-plan church) and found the building already sufficiently repaired to be safe. This cathedral was also damaged in 1667, including its famous portal and bell-towers, but was rebuilt to live on through the most recent shocks. And I felt that the old city was really beginning to breathe again.

It is remarkable to think that there was, even before Edward the Confessor built Westminster Abbey, a Seaman's Guild or Brotherhood in existence in Kotor — as early as AD 809. The nautical museum holds many interesting exhibits; so, too, does the lapidarium. And there are churches, monasteries, a

Kotor's ancient cathedral, now restored and open again

national theatre, delightful small squares, and a splendid clock-tower. All will be restored, one hopes, for at least another 300 years; particularly as each succeeding seismic tremor is lessening in strength, and nothing, it seems, can quench the spirit of this ancient and beautiful city.

There is an old road which climbs up over Mount Lovćen behind Kotor leading to Cetinje, the former capital of Montenegro (see Chapter 5). If you stop to look down on this road from above, you notice that the hair-pin turns below form the letter 'M'. It is also noticeable that those particular hair-pin turns — unlike all the others — appear superfluous on the flatter ground at this point. There hangs yet another romantic story. It tells of the great love that a young Austrian engineer nurtured secretly for Queen Milena, wife of the Montenegrin King Nikola. He dared not show his affection to the Queen, but built her initial into the road he was constructing as a mark of his eternal passion.

Montenegrins don't speak much, these days, about their country's ancient — you might say tribal—customs. But some of these still obtain in the more remote villages, particularly where marriage is concerned. The *kum* or best-man has a much larger part to play than he does in Western Europe. His duty was always to stay with the bride the night before the marriage ceremony to ensure that she was chaste and a virgin. I know one highly respected older man who once had to perform this duty: he assured me he was terrified at the time!

The marriage sheet, too, was traditionally displayed by the bridegroom's mother after the event — couples spent their first night of marriage in his parents' house. There were other lighter-hearted rituals such as the casting of money to the populace by the *kum*. Through the centuries chastity (for women) was considered all-important. Women caught in adultery were stoned, sometimes to death, even to the beginning of this century.

A new road continues along the second side of the fjord, to Tivat, which has its own international airport. Tivat is a local administrative centre; it also has several attractive and informal hotels built as pavilions on the shore.

Close by, there are three small islands. One of them is Sv Marko which has long been used by the Paris-based Club Mediterranée who have built into it all the complex simplicity that this club involves!

The second island is really profuse in cultivated flowers and flowering trees. Called the 'Island of Flowers', there are 60 attractive holiday villas sprinkled about this lush small islet, together with a central restaurant. Tennis courts, bowling and mini-golf are available.

The third island is called Prevlaka and here, too, are villas to rent. In the centre a protected area has been left, with the remains of a ninth-century monastery — Sv Mihailo — together with a nineteenth-century church.

Soon the road, bordered with orange, lemon, grape and peach plantations, leaves the flat lands and soars up to a view of the open sea and one of the most beautiful curving beaches. Called Jaz, this stretch of sandy shore has been left almost deserted until now, except for campers. But there are plans to make this idyllic spot into a sophisticated and high-category tourist centre.

Up on the high cliffs above the sea, the road continues towards Budva and Sveti Stefan; both quite startlingly lovely. Budva, built on a small outcrop of rock, has been a civic centre since earliest times. Although appallingly damaged in the 1979 earthquake, its walls and houses have been restored and it is once more functioning as a tourist attraction.

Sveti Stefan, also on a rock off-shore, was a fishermen's village which in 1952 was turned most imaginatively into a luxury hotel, each cottage forming an hotel suite. In a class of its own, it can hold its head high with luxury hotels the world over.

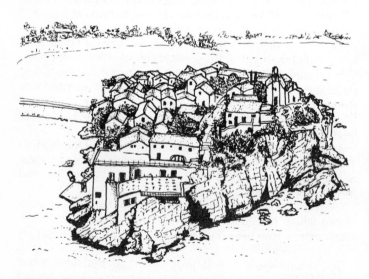

Photogenic in the extreme — tiny Sveti Stefan, fishermen's fortress turned into luxury hotel

It is above Budva that the rock face of the mountains turns from white karst to deep pink — almost terracotta — which heightens an already gloriously picturesque coast.

Budva, according to legend, was founded by Cadmus, son of the Phoenician King Agenor and Queen Telephose. Banished from Thebes, it is said that Cadmus, ruler of Boethia, and Harmonia his wife, found shelter with the Illyrian tribe of Enhelaei. With Cadmus' help, the tribe subjugated their rivals and proclaimed him king of Illyria. It is suggested that the name Budva is a corruption of Boeothia. Socrates wrote that Budva was 'a town in Illyria'. Scylax also mentions it as the capital city of the Enhelaei. Remains found in the necropolis confirm that Budva is one of the oldest settlements in the Adriatic area and was a centre of Bronze Age man. In the fourth century BC it was an Illyrio-Graeco centre, later to become Roman. Pliny wrote that it was 'a town of Roman citizens'. It was a cross-roads of sea and land traffic and trade. When, in AD 395, Theodosius divided the Roman Empire into the Eastern and Western Empires, the southern end of the borderline between east and west ran close to Budva.

It was not until 1938, when the pre-war Hotel Avala was being built at the foot of the steep hill outside the city walls, that the necropolis was discovered, revealing a great deal of information and rich remains. It showed two distinct eras of civilisation. The older Illyrio-Graeco graves of fourth-second centuries BC were 2 m down below the surface. Both sexes were buried in walled graves, together with some of their favourite household objects; steles revealed the names of the dead. The Greek tombs had many ceramic pots glazed in black with red or white decoration. There were also some very beautiful gold ornaments, and two medallions with figures of the cult of Dionysus. The upper level of graves is Roman with a good deal of pottery, many glass objects, including lachrymosas, and coins of both Augustus' and Nero's reigns.

In AD 535 Budva became part of Byzantium and, with the coming of the Slavs and the integration of the original peoples, settled down on a feudal basis. But Stefan Nemanja, the strong Serbian ruler, conquered the whole of Montenegro (then known as Zeta) in 1183, and Budva with it. Later on as power changed hands from one new leader to the next, Budva also changed hands many times, being a valuable prize. It was longest in the hands of the Balšić family who used it as the chief base for their salt trade. Later the Venetians and the Turks vied for its possession.

Through the ages Budva was enriched with beautiful

buildings, both religious and secular. But after the earthquake of 1979 almost none of them remained intact though, miraculously, no one was killed. Now the gigantic task of rebuilding and re-creating the original façades is well in hand: and not for the first time. One of the churches, that of St John the Baptist, was, it is said, originally built in the seventh century and has been reconstructed many times since then.

The Budva Statute of 1371 is a remarkable reminder of just how life was lived in this area in the Middle Ages. Six copies of this Charter have been preserved, and there are 295 articles on the rights of the people. These included legal rights, both criminal and civil, the autonomy of the town, and the proper system of government. There was a Great and a Small council, with a Rector and judges. The Rector was the king's representative, but had to swear allegiance to the Statute. Budva was obliged to supply 50 men under the command of a mounted captain if the king entered into a war in the region between Lake Skadar and Kotor. But the charter also insists on the granting of freedom to fugitive peasants. If a king's man, or one belonging to some nobleman, wished to settle in Budva he was not obliged to serve anyone or any state except Budva itself. A remarkable state of affairs in medieval times, when most of Europe was in serfdom.

Budva was one of the earlier places to realise the potential of tourism. It has superb beaches of coarse sand and many hotels border the sea along the coast. The old Hotel Avala was destroyed in 1979, only to rise again like some phoenix in better plumage. Within two years of the catastrophic quake, a new anti-tremor complex had been built at Slovenska Plaža with arcades of cafés, shops, apartment-style hotel rooms, swimming pools, gardens, sports and entertainment. The Montenegrins, perhaps due to their difficult and warring history, take adversity in their stride and tackle disaster wholeheartedly, turning it into advantage and new success — rehousing their homeless, and using the money that poured in as aid to ensure a better future.

It might surprise some people that a portion of that money was channelled into rebuilding churches and monasteries. But the Yugoslav authorities realise the worth of their heritage, and have an easy secular relationship with the Church which avoids any interference in non-religious affairs.

Perhaps the most poignant result of the earthquake is, for me, on the steep hillside above Sveti Stefan. It is here that the older church of Praskvica Monastery was first built in the eleventh century. When the earthquake struck most of the buildings were almost completely destroyed. The monastery is just above the Magistrala road and I first visited it in 1974. There were then two churches, a museum and an official visiting room as well as living quarters. Several monks lived there together with father Boris the Abbot. After seeing the lovely icons and frescoes in this most peaceful of religious places Iguman (or Abbot) Boris, whose face seemed carved in ivory, offered me Turkish coffee, and we sat at a round dark red marble table to talk. He told me that Queen Milica had sat there 600 years earlier to discuss the affairs of the region. Queen Milica was that tragic and brave queen whose husband and sons had died in the terrible Serbian battle when the Turkish invaders beat the defenders with such appalling loss of life in 1389. The name of that battlefield is forever engraven on the hearts of the South Slav people; it is known as Kosovo Polje, or the Field of Blackbirds.

After the battle Queen Milica went to the field of blackbirds where her dead sons lay and collected their swords. With these weapons she had a lamp fashioned to hang in the monastery church of Dečani. The lamp still hangs there with its soft light — her memorial to that terrible day. But she lived on to administer her lands, even as far south as the Paštrović area around Budva and Sveti Stefan. Her portrait and her name can also be seen on bottles of wine from Serbia. Czarica Milica is one of the most velvety red wines to be found in eastern Yugoslavia.

That first visit to Praskvica Monastery and wise Boris left an impression on me which will last all my life, and it was a great shock to hear how much damage had been done by the tremors of 1979. But when I went back in 1986 there was scaffolding on the crooked walls and the stone flags of the old church were stacked, neatly numbered, in the garden. A monk was there to tell me that the repairs and rebuilding will be complete within two years at the cost of about one million pounds sterling. Iguman Boris, sadly, has departed this life, but his home and his churches, together with the treasures they managed to take away to safety, will be in place again and monastic life will continue as before. The rhythm, temporarily disturbed by disaster, will be as it has been for 900 years and the devastation, in the words of the hymn, will be 'as but an evening gone'.

The tiny island of Sveti Stefan is linked by a causeway built up by the sea and helped by man, providing a splendid swimming beach with calm water on one side or the other — depending on whichever way the wind is blowing. Where the causeway joins the mainland there are two other perfect bays enclosed by rocky tree-covered points — one of them very secluded and still called 'Queen's Beach'. It is here that King Alexander (later to be assassinated in Marseilles in 1934) built his royal summer palace. Now the old house — later used by President Tito when he was in Montenegro — has been renovated and turned into a small luxurious hotel. The gardens are as well kept as ever with roses and wisteria arcades, flowering hibiscus and tree-shaded paths. The old sentry-boxes still guard the gates, though unpeopled. Nearby are two more hotels with equally attractive beaches and excellent service. In particular, Hotel Maestral, though not beautiful on the outside, is all cool marble within; with huge terraces and restaurant, swimming pools, casino and music. It is the service that sets the seal on all good hotels, whatever the category, and it is hard to fault this particular group.

Continuing along the road to the south one arrives at a small sheltered village with a tiny fortress built on a rock at one seaward corner. This is Petrovac-na-Moru — Petrovac-on-Sea. There were many sailors and sea captains born in Petrovac, and it was their habit to bring home foreign trees and shrubs. The village and hillside flaunt gums from the Antipodes and exotic wattles and mimosa, as well as citrus fruit and huge old olives. The hotels are built into this exotic shade, and there is a beautiful beach. Until 1919 the entire village took its name from the fortress, Kaštel Lastva — Swallows' Fort or, I suppose, Swallows' Nest, following the precept that a man's home is his castle!

Beyond the southern extremity of Petrovac is a second beach, Lučica, and there are plans to make use of this very beautiful and deserted stretch of shore for tourism.

Bar, with a huge natural harbour, port and refinery, is close to the south-eastern frontier of Yugoslavia but, before reaching it, you pass Sutomore. As well as several hotels, there are a number of ancient buildings including a chapel first recorded in the eighth century. Between Sutomore and Bar there are two fortifications and a tower where geographical degrees were measured in 1750. One fortress is known as Haj Nehaj. Built, it is said, by the Venetians and strengthened by the Turks, it is an awe-inspiring sight rearing up into the sky. According to popular legend, the Turks ordered all unfaithful women to build these eagle's-nest walls!

From Sutomore to the frontier it is increasingly noticeable how many Muslim people live in the area. Women in oriental dress on the roads and in the fields will often cover their faces in front of passers-by, though they are not obliged to. Men riding on donkeys can be seen in the baggy Muslim trousers of their religion — the fullness being a symbol that the Messiah will be born to a man, not to a woman. Many of the men wear the round white skull-cap which is the sign of Albanian origin, for the frontier is very close. At the same time, there are many other women of all ages dressed entirely in white with raised head-dresses, also in white. This costume is Christian, and very beautiful. There are, perhaps, more examples of this dress in the 1980s than before, due to the friction that has developed between the Albanian majority in Kosovo and the minority of Serbian and Montenegrin families: each, in his costume, declaring his loyalties.

Modern Bar is a sprawling city with blocks of flats, business houses, huge docks, and a very up-to-date hotel called Otrant named after the nearby bay of Otranto.

Ancient Bar, set back on a flat-topped hill, is a mass of early Christian remains. Hardly touched by the most recent earthquake, walls and foundations show many secular and religious buildings, both Christian and Muslim. Unfortunately, the old cathedral of St George, a Romanesque basilica, was used as an ammunition dump and accidentally destroyed in 1881. But a chapel has survived inside the Venetian fortress of the old city together with some Gothic church buildings, and there are the remains of a palace, an aqueduct and some Turkish baths.

It is from Bar that the spectacular new railway runs — through gorges, across rushing torrents and through 254 tunnels — to Belgrade, the federal capital. The line was opened in 1976 and is used for both passengers and freight. So remarkable is the journey that the tourist agencies arrange special excursions on the railway to see the scenery. A much earlier narrow-gauge track used to run between Stari Bar and Vir Pazar, a romantic looking oriental town on Lake Skadar.

Ulcinj, 35 km from Bar, is at the very edge of the Albanian frontier, which is marked by the Bojana River. Ulcinj is even more oriental, especially on Fridays when the country people come in for market day. There have been three cities at Ulcinj: the first fell into the sea in 1444, and the ruins can still be detected; the second, on top of the cliff, has been very badly damaged in the past by another earthquake; and the modern third town still lives, lower down. Even here the more oriental quarter has been very badly damaged by the last earthquake which brought down the oldest and most beautiful of the mosques. This mosque will be rebuilt, but some of the picturesque old Turkish houses with their overhanging screened balconies where the women could sit unseen, are too badly damaged to be repaired.

Ulcinj has many hotels, some on the long fine-sand beach

which continues on the Albanian side, beyond the River Bojana's mouth. Most escaped damage but the oldest, Galeb, with all its old world charm, collapsed completely. In its place the new Hotel Galeb has risen — anti-shock, very well planned and with an excellent kitchen. Apart from the hotel, there are self-catering villas and a good supermarket in the grounds, which slope down under pine trees to the exquisite little rock-bound Ženska Plaža with its sandy beach. Ženska Plaža means 'Women's Beach'. For centuries infertile women have come there to bathe as they believe the sand, sea and iodine have beneficial properties.

Ulcinj was originally called Colchinium and, according to legend, was founded by sailors coming from Colchis on the Black Sea. When the Romans took it from the Illyrians they changed the name to Olcinium from which Ulcinj derives. After Byzantine rule, the town passed through the hands of the Balšić dynasty to Venice until, in the sixteenth century, it was captured by Ulus Ali and 400 of his pirate friends. From then on, for 200 years, it became a stronghold for pirates who lived by attacking ships all over the Mediterranean Sea — even as far west as Morocco. Around that time Ulcinj became notorious as a slave market.

Today there is an open-air market where many ethnic goods such as silver, leather and hand-made rugs are sold. After a little haggling prices are more reasonable than elsewhere and the hand-dyed, hand-woven rugs are especially good buys.

Where the Bojana River broadens out to enter the sea, there is a flat island surrounded by rivulets: Ada island has been turned into a complete nudist complex with houses, pavilions and restaurants separated from the other hotels.

The countryside in this most southerly region seems almost to carry an air of mystery — helped, perhaps, by a strangely opalescent quality of light. Not far inland, across a range of hills, lies Lake Skadar (Lake Skutari or, in Albania, Liqeni Shkodreš).

The Yugoslav/Albanian frontier runs through the middle of this shallow and fascinating lake where the maximum depth is about 6 m and trees, reeds and even horses appear to live in the water, so low and flat are the small sandy islets.

Lake Skadar is a favourite haunt for all sorts of fish, particularly the huge golden carp, and for many kinds of bird. There are egrets and whole families of pelicans that sail, like so many dreadnoughts, on the pearly coloured water. Ponies are taken out to feed on the grass of the islets, and the special flat-bottomed boats are also used for human transport! A causeway runs through the middle of the Yugoslav side of the lake along which you can drive with, at its end, a small hotel used by sportsmen and ornithologists. There are only a few rooms, and the kitchen serves local specialities such as smoked carp which is delicious, and fresh carp — for me, not so interesting — as well as game.

The old town of Scutari at the south-eastern end of the lake now belongs to Albania and is an entry point for that country — if one has all the necessary papers and permissions. At the other end of the lake is Vir Pazar.

The whole region was first inhabited by Illyrians (who have left a necropolis near Vir Pazar) and has changed hands many times. There are numerous old secular and religious buildings including an ancient church built on a trefoil ground-plan, an eleventh-century Orthodox church and, on the island of Vranjina north-east of the town, a thirteenth century Orthodox monastery. On an isolated hill, north of Vranjina, there are the remains of a castle called Žabljak. This castle was the home of the Crnojević family (see Chapter 5, Cetinje) but is not to be confused with the village and plateau of Žabljak in the Durmitor mountain range in the interior of Montenegro. The north-western end of this remarkable lake ends in the river that feeds it near the enchanting small village that takes its name from that river — Rijeka Crnojevića. Though the old, low category Hotel Obod is now closed and awaiting repairs, a journey to this village is well worth the effort for the sheer beauty of the ancient many-arched bridge and its reflection in the still waters. The local population fish for scampi and tiny fish with square nets suspended on flexible rods, throwing the nets down flat on the river bed and raising them when they have a catch, just as they have done almost since time began, and certainly since the Obod printing press nearby was set up in 1493.

C·H·A·P·T·E·R· 2
A Chain of Islands

The entire Yugoslav Adriatic coast has been endowed by nature with a chain of islands, strung like some rich parure just offshore from one end of the country to the other.

The islands as such were formed comparatively recently, as geology goes, when after the last great ice-age the waters rose to form islands where once there had been mountain peaks. This is why the Adriatic Sea surrounding the islands has, for the most part, such depth. The valleys were submerged and now form deep channels of water between the steep slopes of the mountain sides, and straits where the islands are closest to each other.

In all there are about 1,040 islands, including rock reefs, and they are among the most attractive in the northern hemisphere. Many of them are covered in pines and other trees together with a rich variety of maquis and wild flowers. Some of these flowers are endemic to a small area — such as the lily, *Lilium buthuense*, which is found only on the small island of Sv Nikola just offshore from Budva, and takes its name from the original Greek for Budva, Buthue. Fauna is rich and varied. For example, there is a two-tailed lizard to be found on the small island of Biševo just south of the island of Vis. And Korčula island, together with the Pelješac Peninsula close by, is one of the last places in Europe where the small

European jackal can still be seen, and its strange whooping bark heard at night.

About 16 of the larger islands have been developed for tourism. Some others also have private rooms for guests. Of those furthest out to sea, Vis and Lastovo are at present closed to foreign visitors as they are military areas of defence; but there is always hope — and talk — that they may one day be opened again.

Each of the larger islands is quite different in character from the next, due in part to the separate histories of each and the use, through the ages, to which they have been put. All have a wealth of beautiful buildings and other interesting remains. Even the population varies from one island to another, according to the tribes who settled on them and the areas from which those tribes originally came. In some of the islands this fact is even visible from one village to the next in facial features as well as dialect. But perhaps one of the most attractive aspects of these Adriatic islands is the freedom with which they can, with very few exceptions, be visited. They are close enough to each other and to the mainland to be accessible by quite small motor-boats and yachts; and not only are there safe anchorages, but a number of them now have yacht marinas.

THE ISLANDS OF BRIONI

Brioni, since the death of President Tito, is open to the public, and it is possible to visit this small group of two large and several smaller islets either for the day, or to stay in one of the two hotels which were, during President Tito's lifetime, used for special guests and for government meetings. When I visited Brioni, Tito was still living, and I was very conscious of his presence — not as President of the country — but as a man. He loved these islands and could relax there in his rose garden, or when visiting the animals in his small zoo; animals presented to him on state visits to various parts of the world.

There is a small museum arranged inside the walls of an old disused chapel; and many substantial archaeological remains on the island including three Roman temples. First inhabited in pre-historic times, Brioni was later a favourite retreat for the Romans, who built their villas around the shores of the protected coves which slope gently into calm sea. Verige Bay was one of their favourite spots and the remains of a large very elegant villa can still be seen there just above the beautiful blue and aquamarine waterline. Not far from the villa are two huge freshwater cisterns which could each hold 25,000 cubic metres of water; these can still be seen, but one wonders how they were kept topped up. The catchment of rain surely could not have been sufficient.

The main island of Brioni is like a huge park or English estate, with rolling grassland and groups of tall trees. There are asphalted paths wide enough to accommodate an open carriage drawn, when I was there, by two pale grey Lippizaner horses.

Through the ages the islands, being so close to Pula, have provided an enchanting retreat from everyday life for both secular and religious communities and, as early as the sixth to seventh century there was an aisle-less chapel to Sv Petar, the remains of which are still in existence. These days, deer graze peacefully among the trees, there is a large population of hares, and peacocks inhabit the gardens.

In the Middle Ages there was a Benedictine monastery and a basilica on Brioni, but this had to be evacuated in 1312 due to the plague which destroyed so much in Europe. In 1331 the Venetians took control, but later the islands remained almost deserted because of the malarial mosquito which had taken hold of the area in an alarmingly large way. In fact, it wasn't until the nineteenth century that this pest was eradicated after two years of detailed work by the entomologist and bacter-iologist Dr Robert Koch. Then the islands were opened up once more by an industrialist from Merano called Kupelwieser who turned them into an exclusive turn-of-the-century resort, building hotels, swimming establishments, golf links, tennis courts, and even a race track. One of the more famous visitors to this luxury holiday hideout was George Bernard Shaw who knew this part of Croatia well. A day or a week in Brioni is still, after nearly a century, time out from the world, as it was when G.B.S. enjoyed it.

CRES

Time out of a different kind is a visit to Cres — a large island with a huge freshwater lake, and a tiny population. Cres stretches, long and slim in the Kvarner Bay almost due north and south, to be joined at its southern spur by smaller Lošinj. The two islands meet at a narrow junction only a few metres wide at Osor, ancient and legendary city once known as Apsirtides, and mentioned by Apollonius as Apsyrt in the third century BC. This was the place, so legend says, where the Argonauts landed up with Jason and his latest Princess, Medea, when they were chased up the Adriatic by her wrathful father, the king of Colchis.

There are Neolithic cave-dwellings at Punta Križa; Bronze Age and earlier earthworks surrounded by circular stone walls standing at the top of several hills; Iron Age defences; and tumuli. Altogether a small paradise for archaeologists.

Cres, though set in the warmth of a Mediterranean sea, has, strangely, the same rather withdrawn air of the western coast and islands of Scotland and, as you approach one of its small fishing ports from the sea, it can remind you almost of the clear rain-washed look of some Norwegian ports even further north — uncluttered, pale of colour and very clear. Under-populated, it has rolling grassland, small villages, pockets of forest, and the enormous Lake Vrana at its centre whose dimensions seem to increase its mysterious air. Short on hotels, but with many rooms in private houses available, it offers the ultimate in gentle peace.

The biggest of its habitations is also called Cres. In the Middle Ages this municipality took over the administration of the entire group of islands near by, including Lošinj, Ilovik and Susak, from the older centre at Osor when the area came under Venetian rule in about 1459. There are plenty of buildings from this period including the 'City Gate' and clock-tower, and the city loggia (15–16th century). The church holds a really beautiful fifteenth-century pietà and some well-authenticated paintings. The remains of several extensive religious foundations, including a Franciscan monastery and a Benedictine convent, can still be seen.

But Osor is, for me, the most fascinating centre, with its vivid past history. Now living in a backwater, its people are open and charming, with time to spare for visitors.

There are plenty of Illyrian remains about from Osor's earliest inhabitants, and the former medieval town hall now houses a fascinating and very mixed collection of objects — Stone and Bronze Age artefacts, small flat terracotta oil lamps with a decoration of animals or erotic scenes, tear bottles, bones including a Neolithic skull, and a small oblong box made of stone with a lid. This most poignant link with the past still contains the cremated ashes and jewellery from an Illyrian grave.

When the Romans were at Osor the town was a large municipium and trading post between the northern Adriatic ports and Dalmatia further south. To encourage this traffic they cut a canal across the narrow neck of land separating the eastern waters of the Kvarner Gulf from those on the west side, saving the long voyage necessary to circumnavigate the island. Bad luck for the king of Colchis that there was no short cut in Jason's legendary day! Had there been, he would surely have caught up with his wayward daughter. Now, as well as the Roman waterway, there is a second canal with a modern swing bridge.

When the Western Roman Empire fell, Osor was taken over by Byzantium: from the fifth century it became the seat of a bishop. But in 841 the Saracens arrived and set fire to the whole place. In the following century Cres recognised the sovereignty of Croat rulers, but, in the year 1000, it succumbed to the powerful doge, Orseolo of Venice.

In the later Middle Ages Osor gradually sank into comparative obscurity, largely brought on by the ravages of the plague, by malaria, and by a change in the shipping routes as trade and vessel capacity increased. But those earlier prosperous times have left a wealth of rich medieval architecture, including the remains of the sixth-century cathedral and various monastic buildings. There are also the remnants of the Roman town wall, the foundations of a temple, and some mosaics.

Not far up the road from Osor is a small village called Vrana — and, indeed, Vransko Jezero (the lake) — not to be confused with that other Vrana village and lake much further south-east, near Zadar. One way and another, the Yugoslav people do seem to be a little short on names: not only place names — two Vranas, two Žabljaks (both in Montenegro), two Zatons, etc. — but they appear to use far fewer personal names, too. There are so many Djuros, Jurajs (George), Markos, Ivo-Ivan-Jovans (John), Stankas, Petars, Olgas, Gorans and Gordanas, Mihovils and Miškos (Michael), together with a few Željkos and Željkas (wished-for ones), Zlatans and Zlatnas (golden ones) — perhaps as they run out of biblical names. At least they haven't yet taken on the names of Western film starlets! But back to this more northerly village of Vrana and its huge lake.

The village stands above this sheet of water which has a surface area of almost 6 sq km. Lake Vrana lies in a huge bowl on the west side of the island road and hundreds of feet below it. It shimmers, looking almost opaque like mother-of-pearl. The grassland drops down towards its surface interspersed with pockets of deciduous trees, many of them wild cherries. The capacity of the lake is enormous, enough to supply both Cres and Lošinj with fresh water and plenty to spare. It holds 200,000,000 cu m of water in normal times. Its surface is 16 m above sea level, and its bottom lies 68 m below the level of the sea. The water probably reaches the lake by deep underground passages direct from the Velebit mountain range of the Dinaric Alps which lie just inland from the coast between Rijeka and Zadar.

Of a different kind, there is another remarkable sight on the island of Cres. Close to one of the attractive bays is the Valun Stone, dating probably from the ninth century. The fishing hamlet of Valun is on a north-facing wide bay on the western side of the island. And the historically very important stone with its inscription is built into the wall of the sacristy in the little parish church. The writing, on what is thought to be an old tombstone, is the oldest example of the ancient Slav Glagolitic script, and is in the 'obla' form, not in the later 'square' characters. It is important as a carbon-dated witness to the fact that the Slavs were in these islands before they were taken over by Venice.

Cres is so old and quiet with its farming and fishing community that it comes with a shock to cross the isthmus and find oneself in small but giddy sister-island Lošinj.

LOŠINJ

Lošinj is attached to Cres's western side by a mere whisker, to float out like a spare rib for 31 km into the blue sea. And so narrow is it at some points, it seems more like a giant cruise ship than an island. Perhaps it is because the sea is so close on both sides of the narrow island that there is such a lift to the air; this is not only very pleasant, but also beneficial for thoracic complaints and a clinic has long been established at the port and town of Mali Lošinj.

Mali (Small) Lošinj is, in spite of its name, the major town and port of the island. Its harbour, a great natural and almost enclosed basin, is absolutely safe for yachts in all winds. Veli (Big) Lošinj, on the other side of the island, is smaller and not nearly so safe, its harbour mouth being open to the dreaded *Bura* wind from the north-east.

For transportation purposes both Lošinj and Cres are treated as one, with connections from both Rijeka (all the year round), and Brestova on the Istrian coast in summer, fetching up at Porozina in the north of Cres, with road transport down into Lošinj.

Mali Lošinj — in the inconsequential order of things that makes the island so attractive — is the main settlement and has a long maritime tradition, with a nautical school and shipyards, though these declined as modern iron-clads took over from the old graceful wooden ships for which the port was famous. Evidence of this past prosperity is easy to see in the high quality of the stone-built houses surrounding the harbour. In the nineteenth century six shipyards were going strong, providing work and ocean-going ships. In 1870 the Lošinj fleet alone numbered 131 ships with a combined tonnage of 62,000 tonnes. Under Austro-Hungarian rule at that time, the first man to navigate the Cape of Good Hope under the Austrian flag was a sea captain born in Veli Lošinj — his very Slav name was Anton Busanić.

The Hapsburgs favoured Mali Lošinj as a holiday retreat; and one of the most attractive turn-of-the-century mansions there is the 'Villa Karolina' built by the Emperor Franz Josef for one of his favourites. Baroque, and loaded with external decoration, it stands above the beautiful protected Bay of Čikat, surrounded by trees, just over the hill from the harbour.

Though their sea-faring trade inevitably died, Mali Lošinj characteristically did not stop to lick its wounds, but turned wholeheartedly to tourism. It now bristles with hotels, portside cafés and ideas for excursions. Its climate, remarkably warm all the year round, has long held underwater swimming and scuba-diving competitions in winter!

Among one of the most interesting excursions, when weather and water are suitable, are those taken by small boat to other little islands; the two main ones being Ilovik and Susak.

ILOVIK

Ilovik is small, covered mostly with maquis, and sparsely populated. It lies off the southern tip of Lošinj, with a harbour in the form of a narrow channel provided by a tiny islet called Sv Petar. There are prehistoric earthworks here, some medieval ruins, and the remains of yet another *villa rustica*; also a few walls still stand from the eleventh-century Benedictine monastery, Sanctus Petrus de Nembis. In 1597 the Venetians built a fort as part of their defences against the Uskok pirates, so efficient were those heroes of Senj at disrupting Venetian life and trade in the area. Now peace reigns all the year for this small community and their sheep; the only incursions being tourists whom they welcome.

SUSAK

The island of Susak, some 6 nautical miles west of Mali Lošinj, is a phenomenon in the Adriatic. Unlike all the other islands — which are formed of rock — Susak is made entirely of sand and has neither woods nor stones, though bamboos and layer on layer of pre-phylloxera grapes grow there in abundance. The highest point of this 'sand-dune' is 98 m above sea-level, and the island is 6.3 sq km overall. Though entirely made of sand, the island is ringed by rocks which lend credence to one theory that it was formed by volcanic eruption from the sea-bed. The one village climbs up the steep hill from the harbour, the small houses opening directly on to the cobbled street; with an old eleventh-century church and a fortress at the top.

Although Susak has always kept itself very much to itself, its people are remarkably open and friendly, almost untouched by the modern world and its trappings. In the churchyard at the top of the hill only a few family names occur; they have inter-married for centuries with no visible or physical ill-effects. In fact, a medical survey carried out over a number of years on Susak confirmed that its population was particularly healthy!

Because of their isolation, they have preserved their ancient dialect together with marriage customs, dances and songs which are unlike any others. Their women sing directly from the throat with a hard earthy resonance and a nasal intonation far removed from the head singing practised in Western drawing-rooms. The brightly coloured costume, too, is unique. Frequently worn, the mini-skirts of their dress mixes bright green, brilliant pink and chrome yellow, with heavily embroidered borders. The many lace-edged petticoat frills look for all the world like the stiff tutus of the ballerina. With this they wear thick petunia coloured hand-knitted stockings, yellow canvas shoes, white embroidered blouses, and aprons vertically striped with coloured ribbons. Coloured shawls crossed over at the waist and head-scarfs tied at the throat complete this most brilliant of costumes.

Susak has remained poor — still living in a situation when emigration is a sad alternative to unemployment on the home island. At one time drilling for oil near the harbour was carried out. There is gas, but the exploration became too deep to be economic, dashing the hopes of the islanders. Because of its isolated position, tourism has so far passed by this unique island. There is a café; it is used as a kind of village centre and can provide food, drink and Turkish coffee. But don't expect the Ritz: Susak's attractions are not for the plush-minded.

KRK

To the east of Cres and Lošinj and much closer to the mainland, is the far bigger island of Krk. This is the largest island in the Adriatic, though not nearly as long as some others. Its name, like its nature, is uncompromising. Never mind that it has no vowels — just pronounce the three consonants with equal stress and you can't go far wrong; it will sound like the Kirk pronounced in Scotland!

Krk, for hundreds of years, was the headquarters of the powerful Frankopans, a family who influenced events and decisions in Croatia for centuries. They were tough people, and so is the island of Krk. Not for Krk the shy hesitation of nervous village peasants. Old ladies in black will outwit any tourist in finding seats on a bus — amply helped by stiff shopping baskets and furled umbrellas if necessary. They are a cheerful and forthright people; sure of themselves and proud of their heritage and success through history. Proud, too, that they have an international airport on the island which was opened in 1970.

Although Krk is an island, it is now joined to the mainland near Kraljevica by a long bridge with two enormous spans using an islet as footing half-way. This bridge, 1.5 km in length, and 67 m above the sea at its highest point, is a splendid feat of engineering. It was opened on 19 July 1980, and is called Tito's Bridge in his memory. In the last few years it has more or less taken over the job of the old ferries, though there is still a ferry to Šilo from Crikvenica, and in summertime from Senj to Baška at the south-eastern tip of the island.

Although many holidaymakers go to Krk, staying in all parts of the island, the biggest hotel complex is at Omišalj in a completely protected bay. The Haludovo centre includes an 'A' category hotel and several others, plus an attractive 'fishing village' of well-built apartments round an artificially con-structed harbour. Not far away, a second complex has recently been developed at Njivice, only 10 km from the airport.

But to get a more 'authentic' feel about Krk island, it is necessary to go further across it. There are lush fertile valleys high up in the interior between folds of bare limestone rock, and warm green and clear blue horseshoe bays. The colours of the Adriatic sea round the islands are always pure — there is no mauve mixed in to adulterate the blue. Groves of olive trees and vineyards flourish above precipitous cliffs. In spring wild hellebore and cyclamen flower in profusion in the fields, and the tamarisk blossom blows in great clouds of pink.

In Roman times Krk town was called Curicum and, in 49 BC, Pompey's and Caesar's fleets waged a ding-dong battle just offshore. In the Middle Ages the town lay within the protective defence walls and guard towers of the Frankopan residence. The princes lived in the castle from the year 1191. The main tower is three storeys high and you can still climb to the top, with care, and walk along the walls. Hamlet has been performed there before now, in this near-perfect setting.

Though today the population numbers little more than a thousand, in Frankopan times there were twelve times that number, and there are three very old churches all close to each other that were needed to cope with such numbers. The earliest of the churches was a beautifully arched tenth-century building which now acts as crypt for one of the other two.

Apart from a wealth of other medieval buildings in Krk town, there are fragments of delicately carved Roman stone which you come across by accident, let into someone's house wall. Best of all, perhaps, is an extensive and very beautiful black-and-white mosaic floor in a private house. The designs are detailed: two dolphins, some strange sea-serpents, a man with a fish's tail. The owners will sometimes open their door for you to see their priceless flooring.

Punat is only ten minutes away from Krk but, on the way there, you simply have to pause at the roadside to gaze at one of the smallest and most endearing little early Christian churches I have ever seen. Tiny Sv Donat stands alone, a small hump of lumpy stones and mortar with a round dome, a primitive rose-window, a rough hewn porch, and hardly enough room to accommodate six people. Entirely neglected, this small offering touches the heart more than the most grandiose cathedral.

Punat stands at the edge of a shallow bay. There is a small island in the middle of the bay entirely covered by the buildings, gardens and grounds of a lively Franciscan monastery. The brothers welcome visitors and gladly show them round their museum which, as well as housing some beautiful manuscripts, also has some fascinating botanical and biological exhibits though, last time I was there, some of the most lurid of nature's aberrations — such as a two-headed lamb — had been removed upstairs.

Punat was the old seat of the bishops of Krk. There are elegant houses with eighteenth-century stone staircases on the outside walls to first-floor terraces. But it is a sleepy place these days; even the island road peters out there, and life is taken up with fishing and making good the small boats dotted around the lagoon-like harbour. Punat still keeps up its ancient festivals such a the 'dance under the cherry tree' on the first Sunday in May; a festival something like our Maypole Dance; and the 'Puntarska Noć' in August, a tremendous affair with fireworks, decorated 'Viking' boats and a Neptune who rises from the sea! This is very much a tourist night as well, and the wine can be guaranteed to flow.

At the south-eastern tip of Krk a gentle valley slopes down to the sea and to Baška, a delightful village. Baška, too, has ancient roots but its most famous possession is the Baška stone, found in the tiny church of Sv Lucija in the village of Jurandvor, about a kilometre inland. The church, completed in about AD 1100, was built by Benedictine monks on land given by King Zvonimir (crowned by Pope Gregory VIIIth's Legate in 1076). Now the original stone tablet, written in Glagolitic script, is in a Zagreb museum, but there is a good copy still in the church. It records both the gift of land and the building of the church. There was also a polyptich of Sveta Lucija by Paolo Veneziano as an altar-piece but, now that the church is no longer used, this has been removed to Krk town and can be seen in the Bishop's Palace there.

One other town on Krk is remarkable for its difference. Facing north, and set high on the cliffs above the sea, is Vrbnik. It looks across to Senj on the mainland — another stronghold of the Frankopan princes. The people of Vrbnik used to collaborate with the people of Senj in watching the sea for rich Venetian and Turkish prizes.

RAB

Krk's nearest neighbour, Rab, is very different in character but also rich in history and fine architecture. Less than 100 sq km in area, it lies near the mainland, tucked inside the islands of Cres and Lošinj. The next island to the east of Rab, called Pag, is only three nautical miles away on its eastern side.

Rab was first recorded in 360 BC. Its city walls — there are still great portions of them in existence — were built 150 years *prije naše ere* (before our time) as the Yugoslavs call BC. As Arba, the Roman name for Rab, it was a municipal centre in the reign of the Emperor Augustus. The Romans, who had such a good eye for really beautiful places, built villas there as well as naval harbours. Modern Yugoslavia has followed suit. There are many hotels, both near the main harbour and old town of Rab and at the further end of the island overlooking a superb sandy bay. Strangely, you don't see many British people staying in this endearing island, though it is one of the most beautiful, but it is full of other West Europeans.

The early medieval buildings of the small town of Rab really are a joy, with superbly carved stone. The streets are narrow, but the quay is broad and large, and the line boat from Rijeka calls into Rab on its way south to Dubrovnik via Zadar, Split, Hvar and Korčula.

Originally inhabited by the Illyrian Liburnians, the Greeks later formed three settlements. There are some huge stones remaining from those times on the heights above Barbat village and it is well worth making the stiff climb to the top of the hill, called Sveti Damjan, on which the ancient Greek town was located. Then, after the exertion, what could be nicer than to wander down again to a fish restaurant which hangs over the water, its tables shaded by grape vines. These restaurants serve only fresh fish — nothing 'off the ice', or 'Japanese', which simply means from the deep-freeze! Often, the owners keep their stocks in sea-water tanks, both white fish and shellfish such as scampi; nearby there will be mussels hanging on the vertical sisal strands on which they are farmed. *Moules marinières*, *brodetto* (*bouillabaisse*), *rižoto od mušule*, or *škampi na žaru* (grilled on charcoal) are always delicious alternatives to the charcoal grilled or poached white fish that is normal everyday fare in these island restaurants. Another alternative is *Škampi Buzara*: scampi cooked lightly in a superb sauce, which is said firmly by Dalmatians to act as an aphrodisiac.

Through the centuries, life was hard for the people of Rab. For almost 400 years they were under the domination of Venice and, just 47 years after the Venetians had arrived, Rab suffered one of the worst outbreaks of bubonic plague ever recorded. In those days the stern measures taken to try and stamp out disease included burning down houses that were infected, and complete isolation. So, where there is an arch today in one of the main streets of Rab town, at the time of the plague a solid wall was built across closing the town completely to the world. All who were sick lived and died outside the town and that barrier. The chapel of Sv Nikola, near the old loggia, was built in commemoration of this sad period.

But this was not the only tribulation by any means. Her early medieval economy had been healthy, one of the chief industries being the production of silk on the many mulberry trees. A nice legend says that the silk worm was brought back from the east in a hollow bamboo tube by a Rab-born priest. Another industry was the production of olive oil. But the annual tribute demanded by the Venetians in the form of wood was so high that both industries suffered in consequence — without trees, no silk and no oil. Their fish-preserving industry, too, shrank to almost nothing at that time. The Venetian salt monopoly made it far too expensive for Rab to buy salt and, though surrounded by the very salt Adriatic Sea, they were precluded from obtaining their own.

Even in the twentieth century Rab was still suffering. After World War I the island, like Rijeka (Fiume), was occupied from 1918 by Italy until, after the treaty of Rapallo in 1920, the island finally became a part of the kingdom of Yugoslavia.

In spite of — perhaps because of — those hard facts, the people of Rab are gentle and friendly; kindly, and with time to spare when help is needed. The island has an air of timelessness in its everyday life. And its beautiful protected bays seem to echo the fact that life is for peaceful living, away from the bustle of Rijeka and the rush of the world.

PAG

Last in this north-western group of islands, and before the beginning of Dalmatia proper, is the long thin island of Pag. Except for its north-western tip which is on the further side of a steep crest, Pag is as different from Rab as chalk is from cheese, or sheep from goats, though, curiously, these all seem very relevant to Pag. For this seemingly barren island is famous for its cheese, its hand-made lace, and its chalk-like surface which is, in fact, bare karst rock looking, when viewed from a distance, very much like the chalk downs of southern England. Pag is the island which most strongly feels the force of the *Bura* wind in winter. Because of its geographical position off-shore below the Velebit range of the Dinaric Alps, the wind blows down on it with great strength, picking up salt and depositing it on the north-facing slopes. Vegetation is so sparse that the karst rock has a chalky look — tinged, in the pure air of dawn and sunset, with a pale ethereal pink. But that sparse vegetation is entirely suitable for the sheep from whose milk Pag cheese is made. This hard strong-flavoured cheese is famous throughout Yugoslavia. It is used both for *hors d'oeuvres* (*predjelo*) and for grating into sauces and on pasta.

As a cottage industry the women of Pag make pillow-lace in beautiful traditional designs, and they can be seen in cottage doorways when the sun is shining, busy at their craft. When in their national dress, this lace is used on their high starched head-dresses, and they make runners and cloths and mats of it too.

Pag is not very big, just very long and thin. It is underdeveloped as a holiday island but there are some hotels and some private rooms, as well as camping sites. The oldest of the small towns is Novalja, which was a Roman naval base. Earlier, it was an Illyrian settlement from which time there are burial grounds and fortifications. The bay in which Novalja lies faces the open sea but, on the landward side and only 3 km away, there is another long protected inlet with Caska at its head. This early centre was destroyed by earthquake in AD 361 when part of it fell into the sea. From the old settlement there are still the remains of buildings, an aqueduct, an acropolis and, most important, the domestic altar, or *ara* of Calpurnia, the daughter of Lucius Piso, a Roman consul who took refuge on Pag when in trouble with Rome in about 20 BC. Don't confuse the old buildings, though, with the high tower on a circular base; this is a nineteenth-century addition which is used by tunny fishers as a look-out when the fish are running!

The people of Pag believe that the word *pagus*, meaning a source of water, comes from the ancient Greeks who stopped off there. There are several freshwater springs on the island — at Novalja, Pag town and Metajna.

During the Middle Ages this long slim island was carved up by various rulers. In 1071, for example, King Peter Krešimir handed half over to the bishop of Rab, and the south-eastern part to Zadar. Gradually, Old or *Stari* Pag took over from Novalja as the civic centre, and from then on began to don its cloak of fine buildings. In the thirteenth-century, after many changes of ownership, King Bela IVth made Pag a free royal city on 30 March 1244 in recognition of the help he had received in quelling the Tartar hordes of Ogodai.

Pag became rich from her salt-pans, her cheeses and her olive production and, when the original town was burnt down to cleanse it from the plague, the 'new' town of Pag was begun in 1443 on the other side of those salt-pans which, even these days, still form the town's main industry. It was here in the new town that the famous stone-mason, Juraj Dalmatinac, began the beautiful cathedral which took 80 years to complete. He was also responsible for the bishop's palace, and the palace of the Podesta in the main square.

The south end of the island is now joined by a bridge to the mainland near Zadar. The other end, with its sleepy village of Lun, is close to the island of Rab, and once belonged to that island. In fact, Lun boats are still registered in Rab.

THE KORNAT ISLANDS

Looking south and east from Pag the map shows an almost incredible scatter of small islands, many uninhabited, stretching just offshore from Zadar as far as Šibenik. The Kornat group of islands numbers in hundreds and is quite beautiful to see, whether viewed from the air or the sea. From the air the islands appear almost as drops of water spilt on a polished surface. Most are sparsely covered with grass and a little scrub but with few trees. Local farmers row out their sheep in summer to feed on these islands, fetching them home in autumn to winter on the mainland or on the bigger islands. Much of the Kornati area has been made into a marine national park in order to preserve the flora and fauna on both land and sea. It is delightful to wander by boat slowly (a speed of more than five knots is forbidden) from one tiny island to the next in the clear air and on such calm limpid water.

Of the bigger islands, the first is Ugljan, just opposite Zadar and about 1.5 km from the mainland shore. Here the water is shallow and calm enough for small boats to commute between Zadar and the village of Preko — which simply means 'across' — and other small villages and ports. Ugljan is almost joined at one end to Pašman, the next sizeable island, which also has a road on its landward side, and several small villages and harbours. Further out to sea, and parallel to the other islands, is Dugi Otok (Long Island!), with a number of other smaller islands scattered around. There are one or two newly built hotels on the bigger islands, but they are mostly used by Yugoslav families rather than by foreigners. In Yugoslavia the annual holiday is taken very seriously and, from all areas inland, there is a general exodus — once the schools have closed in summer — either to the sea or to the mountains and lakes. Many of the bigger Yugoslav firms own hotels and big guest houses along the coast to which their employees and their families can go for their holidays at reasonable cost. But many Yugoslavs like to 'go-it-alone', preferring to meet people outside the parameters of their work. Many others, in summer, visit their family homes to help with the vineyards, and generally lend a hand.

Further on towards the mainland town of Šibenik there is Murter; small, and so close to the mainland, that it is a commuter suburb. Here, at the little port of Betina, there is a long-established wooden ship-building industry. Many of the large old sailing ships now used for group cruising among the Adriatic islands started out in life from Betina at the turn of the century.

Outside the mouth of the Krka River among many other small islets, lies Zlarin with an attractive cluster of houses round its port. Zlarin is distinguished for its unusual industry, and is known as 'Coral Island'. For generations the men of Zlarin have gone to sea, using the knowledge and unpublished charts of their forefathers to lead them to the best coral grounds. When they returned their women folk polished and fashioned the coral into jewellery. Their tools were primitive but effective, and there is a small museum in the village of Zlarin which shows just how patiently the work was carried out.

On the further side of Šibenik there is another, even smaller island called Krapanj. Krapanj, too, has a remarkable industry. Very close to the mainland, Krapanj's only village straggles along the length of its inner seaboard. The stone houses are well built and, if you land there, you will probably see only women and children and old men. For the younger active males of the families will be away at sea. Their industry is sponge-diving and, like Zlarin, they work on knowledge gained from their fathers and grandfathers. Sponge-diving, like diving for coral, is hard on health and lungs, but there are still those willing to carry on the old tradition: sponges fetch a good price.

ČIOVO

South of Primošten the myriad Kornati islands peter out, and as one nears Split, some bigger islands come into view. First are the underdeveloped islands of 'Small' and 'Large' Drvenik; then, close to the mainland and actually joined by a bridge to Trogir is Čiovo.

Like Murter, Čiovo is both a commuter island and, more recently, a favourite place for Yugoslavs to build their weekend cottages. It is not highly developed for tourism, but has some interesting buildings and a past history that delves back into legend. In fact one theory is that the ancient Greeks gave the island its original name of Bua, or Boa. Bua means a place of snakes, though you would be hard put to it to see one now. But legend has it that these creatures were constrictors large enough to attack the cattle and devour them.

Later, in the days of the Roman emperor Diocletian, the island was used as a place of political exile. Later still, it was completely uninhabited except for a few hermits. Then, in about 1214, a Franciscan order of brothers made their monastic home there.

Čiovo is a small island overshadowed by Trogir, but it had its uses when danger threatened the people on the mainland. Roads fan out from the bridge connecting the island to Trogir, and there are six small villages. For lazing and sailing Čiovo is ideal, and there are some old buildings worth visiting including an early Romanesque chapel, and the fifteenth-century church and Benedictine monastery at the village of Sveti Križ (Holy Cross) on its southern shore.

ŠOLTA AND BRAČ

South of Čiovo and opposite Split (giving that great port complete protection from southerly winds) are the twin islands of Šolta and Brač, almost joined at the *Splitska Vrata* — a narrow seaway through which the bigger ships go gingerly. Šolta is small and quiet, a delightful island on which to wander at leisure. It has several inland old-world villages and three beautiful protected deep bays. Two of these bays face north towards the mainland; the third faces west, and is proof against the *Bura* wind.

There is a fertile central valley on the island where a lot of grapes are grown for wine and, in the sheltered inlet of Rogač — one of the north-facing coves — there is a village with an interesting industry. This is the harvesting of locust beans from the carob (or *rogač*) trees which grow to a great height there. The beans, in their black ripened pods, are gathered and then processed into a protein-rich flour which is made into a baby-food. These are the same beans as are occasionally found, intact in their dark pods, in health food stores.

Though Šolta may be quiet and far less known to visitors than Brač, it is not short on history. It was first recorded four centuries BC by Pseudoskylax when it was called Olynthia. Illyrians and Romans left their mark and, when the Avars destroyed the city of Salona (now the district of Solin, just inland from Split) in AD 614, many of the refugees from that city fled to Šolta and, from that time, its affairs were closely connected with Split. During the Middle Ages it was variously under attack by pirates from Omiš, and the Venetians. But the population of the island increased further when, in 1537, the fortress and settlement of Klis fell to the Turks. Now the only invasion is in summer when fugitives from the world of commerce seek rest and shelter along its quiet hospitable shores.

Brač is the third largest island in the chain (with almost 400 sq km) and also the highest. It is famous for its quarries which yield some of the densest and whitest stone — for building and for carving — that is known. Brač stone, like that of a much smaller island, called Vrnik and close to Korčula, is famous all over the world. It has been shipped to the USA and to England. It was used in Paris to build the Sacré Coeur, and it forms the altar stone of the new Liverpool cathedral; the doorway of the United Nations building comes from Brač and so does stone in the White House in Washington. Though they have been in use since the Romans were in Split, the quarries are still working, and a floor of polished Brač or Vrnik stone is, in this warm area of the world, still preferable to parquet or tiles, and just as smooth.

Brač stone is either shipped or carried to the mainland on lorries, crossing the straits to Split on the big car ferries. It is fascinating to see them load, on a roll-on roll-off open ferry system, together with local pedestrians streaming among them with their baskets for the morning's shopping — everyone jostling to get away quickly, either to or from the island. There are different ferries for each island and most of them carry a relevant name — such as 'Lastovo I', 'Bračanka', etc.

The most popular tourist resort on Brač lies on the south side, facing the island of Hvar and called Bol. All the islands in this part of the Adriatic lie east and west and overlap each other. Bol has the protection of Brač's mountain, Vidova Gora, behind it, and the island of Hvar as a protective shield in front. The port of Bol is enchanting, with a miniature harbour for its small boats, honey-coloured stone houses — including the Venetian palazzo that acts as post-office — and a great air of intimacy. Specially loved by the British, the hotels are to the side of the little town and spaced out under pine trees on a level area of fertile land by the sea. The shore is quiet and sunny with, on one side, the famous Zlatni Rat (or Golden Point), a long horn of shore jutting out into the sea, built up by the currents. This horn is flat and pale golden in colour with, where land meets sea, the most startling hues of yellow, pale green, aquamarine and deepest blue as the depth increases. So attractive is it that artists paint and photographers feature Brač's 'Golden Horn', while bathers are assured of calm sea on one side or the other, according to the wind.

There is a delightful small Dominican monastery on the shore between hotels and town where the monks have, over the years, got together an interesting museum. Founded in 1475, the church with its gothic vaulting was later enlarged, and the monastery contains a number of works of art. Among the items on show are some Stone Age knives and flint tools, medieval manuscripts, and a vast quantity of coins, each one a key to Brač's long history. The islanders have always been primarily an agricultural community with, even today, about 10,000 sheep as well as cattle. Through the centuries power was always in the hands of the working landowners, who bred their livestock, living on their secluded estates. Even today there are a few horses breeding on the upland pastures.

Brač is a prime example of how history has dominated and differentiated around the islands. There are, among the villages, two distinct dialects — known a *ča* and *ca* — according to where mainland refugees landed and from whence they came. Even between one village and the next, the dialect varies considerably; and the features of the inland villagers on the island are different from those on other islands — or from those of the once Venetian-dominated ports. In early times all communities settled for safety in the hills, unseen from the sea, and those early villages still form the heart of the Brač community.

It is fascinating to cross the island from the port of Supetar, climbing over the mountain to Bol on the other side: up from sub-tropical vegetation at sea level, through lavender plantations and groups of morello cherry and mulberry trees, peaches and almonds (all grown commercially), to upland — almost alpine — pastures, before dropping down again into the heat at sea level. Half-way across one arrives at Nerežišća which has some lovely old buildings, as well as fragments from Roman times. This quiet little village was once the municipal centre of the island, though it has long since been overtaken by Supetar with its good harbour. It is here that four roads meet, leading to other villages and to the heights of Vidova Gora (778 m), the dramatic mountain rising gradually through uplands on the north side, and falling suddenly down to the sea near Bol. At the top-the flowers are sub-alpine, growing in the short thick grass close to the soil. There are wild thymes, mountain sage, saxifrage, juniper, campanulas, honeysuckle and coltsfoot, and a myriad other small star-like pink and yellow blossoms with their faces firmly turned skywards.

A cautious walk to the edge of the mountain's south face reveals the Adriatic and its islands like a relief map. There, spread out, are Vis and Lastovo, Hvar and Korčula, and, further towards Dubrovnik, the huge thin peninsula of Pelješac, so nearly but not quite an island. The drop from Vidova Gora is sheer, almost 800 m down to Zlatni Rat below.

Brač has a good deal to offer, and there are organised excursions in summer to the other islands and the mainland. It is a far cry from the dark days of war which many villagers still remember — including one elderly man who told me that, aged only 14, he was shot at by the enemy but the bullet went through his hat. He lay still for hours until it was safe to move! Nos 40 and 43 British Commandos were in action on Vidova Gora. They arrived from Vis and fought with great courage and, sadly, many casualties, with Tito's Partisans, fighting their way to liberate the mainland.

VIS

Vis, one of the furthest islands from the mainland, lies almost due south of Split. Only 90 sq km in area, Vis is not elongated like the islands close to the mainland, but compact and hilly with its highest point 587 m above sea-level. There are two ports, one facing north-east, called Vis — the administrative centre — and the other facing south-west and called Komiža. From 1969 the island of Vis was open to foreigners for a few years. But it has always formed a kind of forward defence post for Yugoslavia, and it was later closed once more. It *is* possible for people of other nationalities to visit the island, but anyone wishing to do so must first obtain a permit.

Vis is not only a very beautiful island but, historically, extremely interesting, being one of the first to be colonised by very early Greek settlers who knew it as Issa. Those Greeks, like the Illyrians before them and the Romans who came later, left for posterity some outstanding examples of the art of that time: exquisite small figurines, such as that depicting the two pulls of 'Love and Soul' — Love being shown as a woman of motherly proportions, and Soul as a young boy, half way to manhood. There are some small tanagra figures there, too, and one outstanding bronze head of a Greek goddess, possibly Aphrodite, as well as fine quality vases and glass phials. All these treasures are up on the first floor of the museum, while the ground floor is devoted to pictures, newspaper cuttings, weapons, etc., from the war of liberation. At one point during the war Vis was the only place free from the enemy occupiers.

It was in Vis that Tito and his Partisan forces landed when Bosnia was finally overrun. To Vis, also, came the British Commandos. Gazing at those wartime photographs on the walls of the museum, one finds oneself searching for the faces of old friends who were on the island at that time.

The people of Vis remember those times as if they were yesterday. My most recent visit was two years ago, when we were privileged to accompany a number of veterans of 43 Commando for the 40th anniversary of their involvement. The welcome was almost unbelievable in its warmth; and stories of those stirring times flowed as freely as the excellent Vis wine, *Vugava*, and Vis's specialities in the way of food. It was a wonderful day, full of mutual affection.

But World War II was not the only time the British were on Vis in strength. During the Napoleonic wars the British navy, with shore batteries and ships under the direction of Admiral

The exquisite head of a Greek goddess, perhaps Aphrodite,
found in Vis

Fremantle, together with Captain William Hoste, were there
for three years (1811–14) to break the French blockade of
Europe. There is a British cemetery from those times on one
arm of Vis harbour which is still carefully tended. Four of the
defence forts round the harbour still bear their English names
— George, Wellington, Bentinck and Robertson — though
they are not all still intact.

Both Vis and Komiža are rich in medieval stone houses and
churches, some of outstanding beauty. And the entire island is
scenically very attractive, with a rich cultivated central valley
(ploughed up during the war to make a landing strip).

The highest point of the island is Mount Hum, in the
south-west. Near the top are some caves with rough steps
leading up to them. Here Tito and his HQ staff lived and
worked during his months on Vis. One cave acted as his
Cabinet and War Room; one as his bedroom; and a third small
recess was reserved for his beloved guard dog 'Tigger'. Now

these caves are almost a place of pilgrimage for old and young Yugoslavs alike.

Just off the port of Komiža there is the small island of Biševo (5.8 sq km) which is remarkable for three things. One is its spectacular 'Blue Grotto' which, when entered, shows every-thing in a dazzling blue light. The second is another grotto called Medvidina, from the Croat word for seal. Seal mothers use this cave to rear their young, and the species is protected by law. The third unique fact is that Biševo has, in common with two other far-out islands, a species of lizard which is black in colour and carries a double, or forked tail.

Its isolation from the bigger world has kept Vis back from material progress. But it has also preserved the island and its people as they have been for generations. They are intensely generous, and interested in any new faces that appear — even for a day. Nothing is too much trouble, and their kindness seems infinite. Any excuse seems good enough for the wine from Vis's own factory to appear.

Besides the production of wine, fish for canning, and early vegetables, there is a nursery garden specialising in producing Phoenix palms, *Phoenix canariensis*. Close to the wine factory, the nursery is run by the same management. Recently a new and attractive holiday hotel has been built against the time when Vis may be once more open to the outside world. They have a large safe harbour in Vis town, though not in Komiža which is open to the Southerlies. Communications are good with a daily ship from Split. All they need is permission for foreign visitors.

LASTOVO

The island of Lastovo, like Vis, is closed to foreigners at the present time, and for the same reasons. Much smaller than Vis — only 52 sq km — it, too, is compact. But it has its own small archipelago of 46 tiny islands, mostly uninhabited. The fishing grounds are rich with lobster-sized crayfish, as well as some of the best white fish in the Adriatic.

Lastovo lies out to sea a few nautical miles south of Korčula with its three mountainous humps hiding the little town — also called Lastovo. In the Middle Ages it was rich with many families from Dubrovnik living there in considerable style. Together with Pelješac, Lastovo was an outpost of the Dubrovnik Republic, and opposed to Venetian Korčula which lay between the two. These days, the busiest part of the island is on its south-west coast at Ubli where there is a perfectly protected harbour approached from the west, and a road leading across the island to the older town. There is one hotel near Ubli called (appropriately) Hotel Solitudo which has recently been rebuilt to up-to-date standards.

A great deal of the island is covered in magnificent trees and, where terraces that supported wine grapes have been deserted due to economic difficulties, a rich variety of maquis and wild flowers run riot. I was once there in October and saw a mass of autumn cyclamen and yellow 'crocus' (*Sternbergia lutea*) under arbutus bushes dripping with dark red sun-ripened fruit — like so many Chinese lanterns hung for a festival.

Lastovo still preserves its rich national costume and its carnival when, traditionally, a whole scriptless play is performed on the cobbled streets of the old secluded town. The features of Lastovo people are distinctive, and the women are very good looking with short, rounded features. Their national dress includes a skirt of fine black wool with almost accordion pleating, which is carefully preserved in ancient wooden chests for special days.

There is little prosperity in the island nowadays, though a benign government sees to it that special concessions — such as very cheap transport — ease the economic strain imposed on it.

Lastovo is one of those rare places so attractive in its loneliness that, while half of one hopes it will find a new prosperity in tourism, the other half desperately wants it to remain just as it is: gentle, shy, and withdrawn from the brash new world.

HVAR

Approaching the island by ship the first sight of Hvar and the exquisite medieval buildings of the port and town bearing that name, is almost incredibly beautiful. And the fact that you cannot land a car off the ferry at this point is aesthetically an advantage, though it may be tiresome, practically speaking. Among the first things to meet the eye are the arched Venetian arsenal where the galleys of war used to wait, ready floating; the very grand old loggia; the superb façade of the count's palace, now an hotel; and the delicate balustrade with its obelisks that surrounds the original inner harbour. The carving of windows and door lintels on the old houses is intricate and of fine quality. There are palm trees where the ships dock, and delicate church campaniles in the distance. Round a corner is a huge square — the biggest in Dalmatia — paved in white stone with, at an outer corner, one of the oldest and most beautiful little theatres in Europe. It was opened in 1612, while William Shakespeare was still alive, and still has the tiers of dark red curtained boxes lining two-thirds of the walls, as well as an auditorium filled with seats. The acoustics are remarkable, and the theatre is still sometimes in use. The smell of grease-paint is strong, and some of the plays performed there stem from early poets and playwrights of Croatian literature. For Hvar had a rich, highly educated patrician hierarchy.

The port faces south with some outlying islands (the Pakleni) protecting its entrance. The hills behind the town rise very steeply with, on their tops, two fortresses. The Austrians, during their nineteenth-century occupation, enlarged the bigger of these massively built strongholds. It is now in use as a series of attractive terrace restaurants, and a disco — well above the town — so that the early rising residents can sleep. For Hvar's population, in common with all Dalmatians, believes in rising early — starting work at 6 am or earlier in the fields, or 7 am in the offices and shops.

Hvar took hold of tourism for a living with both hands, about a century ago. It runs the industry very efficiently and has many hotels on the island to accommodate the big influx of guests who flock there each summer. And it has learnt to speak, perhaps, more of the German language than the British. Hvar has many advantages to bolster up its tourist industry. Facing south, its main centre can boast a warmer climate than some other islands. And for years, as a publicity stunt, it has offered a refund if there is snow (hardly ever!) or more than three hours of rain in a day during the summer months (very unusual!). Another advantage is its nearness to Split and the airport, and its ease of communication with the mainland: by ship; by hydrofoil; by motor launch; or by smaller car-ferry to three different locations on the island where it is possible to land a car.

One of these latter ports is Stari Grad (Old Town) which was in fact the earliest — 384 or 383 BC — habitation known to the Greeks. They called it Pharos (a light).

On the hills above Stari Grad and the other small ports on this side of Hvar there are some huge 'Cyclopean' stones still in evidence where those early settlers built dry walling. It is thought that they staged at Pharos on their way up the Neretva River to Bosnia, and further to the Danube, the Black Sea, and even to the Baltic and the Amber Route.

Certainly Hvar was not a 'new place' even then. It has been continuously inhabited since early man used Stone, Bronze and Iron Age tools, some of which can be seen today in the museums, together with early ceramic art, and adornments such as the famous *armilla*, fashioned in copper.

At sea level in the centre of Stari Grad there is the fifteenth-century residence of one of Hvar's most humane medieval figures. He also owned the beautiful palazzo in Hvar town of which only the outside walls still stand. Petar Hektorović was a writer and poet who lived from 1487 until 1572 — a long life for a man in those days. His house in Stari Grad is massive. It was built on low vaulted arches set on rectangular stone pillars and it occupies one entire side of the square in the town. It has a garden with cloisters and a large oblong fish-pond which still teems with grey mullet. There is fresh water running into the fish-pond as well as salt water which arrives through a channel from the sea. Even in those early times they knew that the delicious grey mullet (or *Cipal*) live best in a mixture of fresh and salt water, just as oysters do. Petar Hektorović allowed beggars and down-and-outs to use one side of his cloisters when they were homeless, but only for three months at one time, lest they should become too soft.

Further east on this deeply indented coast, and close to each other, are two inlets with the fishing ports of Vrboska (willowy), and Jelsa (perhaps from *Jalsa*, the alder tree). Both names give a hint that here is the one sizeable source of spring water on the island; enough to supply its normal needs.

Both Vrboska and Jelsa have good natural harbours: Jelsa's being rounded with a sandy beach at one side, and Vrboska's having a long slim inlet of deep water, sufficient for the needs of the old sailing ships. The outer arm is densely wooded with a large hotel among the trees.

Both little settlements have modern hotels and ancient houses, and both have fascinating fortified churches. In the fifteenth-century, when the Ottoman Empire was threatening to overrun the Adriatic, the two churches — Sv Sebastian, and Sv Marija — were fortified and, in addition, had huge cisterns for water built in, so that the sheltering inhabitants could stay inside the defending churches for considerable periods. Near Sv Marija at Vrboska there is a second church, Sv Lovre, which now houses some fine pictures — some of them brought from the older church — including works by Titian, Veronese, Bassano and two by the Dubrovnik painter, Celestin Medović.

Hvar was in rich company from early medieval days, and is justly proud of its heritage. The people are energetic and enthusiastic, keen business people, whether it is in tourism that they work or — as in the case of the old ladies selling lavender oil at the port — on their own affairs. This lavender oil, of very pungent quality, is almost synonymous with the name of Hvar, for the country people for centuries have cultivated this aromatic plant on the slopes of the hills. In summer those hills look as if covered in a blue mist above the limestone rock and red soil. Another industry is the production of pyrethrum dust as an insecticide from the flowers that grow wild. But, by and large, Hvar has given itself and its treasures to tourism. Treasures which include the vast painting of 'The Last Supper' — *Tajna Večera* — which hangs in the refectory of the little Franciscan monastery to one side of Hvar harbour. Hvar has a lot to offer as a holiday island, and it is not surprising that visitors arrive, summer and winter, from all parts of Europe and Scandinavia.

Korčula

The island of Korčula lies parallel with Hvar, overlapping it for about two-thirds of its length. At the same time it accompanies the last slim portion of the Pelješac Peninsula. Indeed, the sea channel here is only 1,200 m across at its narrowest.

There are three ways of approaching this very lovely island: by boat from Split to its western port of Vela Luka; by ship from Split or Dubrovnik to the port of Korčula town — the island's main administrative and cultural centre at the eastern end of the island; or by motor-launch from Orebić (on the Pelješac Peninsula to Korčula town). The latter two routes provide the greatest impact; a feast for the eyes that is hard to beat for ethereal beauty.

At first sight the richly endowed medieval walled city, small as it is, seems to float on the deep limpid blue sea, completely covering the rocky pinnacle on which it was built for safety,

Korčula, a small poem in stone, seems to float on the azure sea

originally with a moat on the landward side. The massive walls and corner towers of the city reflect with a mirror image in the water when the sea is still and, within the walls, the old houses climb the narrow streets which rise — on a fishbone plan — up to the main square and the cathedral. The bell tower of Sv Marko is a poem of delicate stone which rises high enough to act as a navigation point on the admiralty charts of the area. The cathedral itself is a small masterpiece of fifteenth-century architecture with some particularly interesting carved figures above its main portal. The square also holds the bishop's palace with a church treasury; the main museum in an old patrician palace; the carved stone column which formerly carried the standards and from which proclamations were made; and another carved stone pillar used for minor punishments, known as the whipping post.

Korčula, altogether, has 17 churches. There are two entrances to the city; the oldest is by a beautiful flying staircase, its balustrades carved in stone, which enters through the oldest gateway and fourteenth-century tower, dating from 1384. The other, also a stairway, lies on the west side of the walls and leads up from the old quay (where most of the cruise ships dock) and past the loggia, once used by the city elders, which has now been skilfully adapted as a tourist office.

Inside the walls, many of the old Venetian palazzos are still occupied, split up into flats; many others are roofless as a result of the plague. One of the biggest of these patrician dwellings was the Arneri palace which occupied an entire street leading to the cathedral in its heyday. One end of this is still lived in by the family. The other end is, even now, undergoing renovation to be made into a museum, with the aid of money donated by an American benefactress, and the deeds given over jointly by the Korčulan family and the local town hall.

The Arneri (or Arnerić) family were prominent in the island for generations; the last head of the family, Juraj, entertaining several kings. There was Edward VIIIth among others, who cruised down the Adriatic in 1936 on the yacht *Nahlin* with Wallis Simpson — later Duchess of Windsor — and Lady Diana Duff Cooper. Rebecca West was another visitor when she wrote *Black Lamb & Grey Falcon*. The Arnerić family are still respected in the island.

Among the houses, almost hidden and on the ground floor, are a number of jewellery shops while, just outside the walls, is a whole line of stalls selling cheaper souvenirs. Near the flying staircase the wide stone rotunda teems with country women selling fruit and vegetables; shouting to each other, and to fascinated tourists.

Between the city and the tourist hotels, on the old road by the sea, there is a semicircular rotunda with entrance pillars resembling miniature Cleopatra needles on which the Latin inscription is still clear. This states that the paved area with its stone benches was given as a solarium by the British to the people of Korčula in appreciation of their kindness and hospitality during the Napoleonic wars. Under Col. Peter Lowen, a British garrison was stationed on Korčula for two years. In 1813 they built the road that leads up, past the fifteenth-century Dominican monastery of Sv Nikola, to the hill of Sv Vlaho which dominates the town and straits. At the top they constructed a round three-storeyed fortress with emplacements on the flat roof for heavy naval guns. With these they commanded the straits — one of the most important seaways during that time of European blockade. Today the path and stone steps still lead to the tower which now sports a television repeater aerial on its roof. From time to time a snack-bar is opened on the ground floor, but often the building is empty. In either case, the walk up through the pine trees is very well worth while: the views of sea and islands are memorable.

The island of Korčula is 48 km long and, in most places, about 8 km wide. It is hilly and richly covered in pines, cypresses and lush Mediterranean shrubs such as arbutus, myrtle, juniper and holm oak, together with cistus, rosemary, cytisus, anchusa, iris and herbs like oregano and mountain sage. So lush is the vegetation that the ancient Greeks called the island Korkyra Melaina, 'Black Korkyra' (or Corfu) when they first approached it about 6 centuries BC. Neolithic man and the Illyrians lived there for centuries before that time and, along the central road that runs the length of Korčula island to Vela Luka, there is still visible evidence of those early people. Only a few metres from the roadside as you approach the highest village, Pupnat, there are small pyramids of stones which are tumuli marking the graves of Illyrians who were buried, with some household goods, in a sitting position — untouched until the present day.

It was the Greeks who first colonised Korčula in a big way, about three centuries BC. They even left a stone tablet listing the names of some of the settlers and mentioning their occupations.

A journey through the length of the island on the local bus takes in all the main small habitations. There is Žrnovo, Pupnat, Čara and Smokvica (the latter two being the main

centres for growing the sought-after pale white wine, *Pošip*);
then Blato, near the further end of the island; and finally Vela
Luka. Each village has something to offer in the way of old
churches, a well-known triptych, or a beautiful loggia. Some
villages — like Žrnovo and Blato — have an ancient
dialogue-and-costume pageant which has been enacted for
centuries on special occasions. Between all these villages the
land rises and falls in steep parabolas covered in huge pine
trees. But along the middle of the island there is a fertile
central valley intensively cultivated with vines.

At the far end of the island the land slopes more gently
down to the sea and the big harbour of Vela Luka which lies
protected by two long arms of land covered in trees and
maquis. Vela Luka has long had a fish canning factory, and
now has a substantial plastic-boat building yard as well as five
hotels, including the new high category Adria Hotel, just
opened. This imaginatively built hotel at the water's edge has
a fully equipped medical centre for thoracic complaints and
the rehabilitation of open-heart surgery patients.

The area around Vela Luka has long been known as
beneficial for rheumatic diseases. The actual name 'Blato'
means mud, and an older hotel and clinic makes use of the
radio-active mud which seeps down to the sea at one corner
of the huge natural harbour.

There is a museum these days, and one of the items is a
Henry Moore sculpture which he presented to Vela Luka to
help the little town in 1978 when it suffered much damage
from a freak tidal wave.

Any pastimes in this gentle corner of Korčula are leisurely,
and mostly involve boating, bathing and fishing. But the
Romans were there, and some mosaic flooring can be seen if
you walk round the point beyond the new hotel. Neolithic
cave men were there even earlier, and some lived in Vela
Špilja (Big Cave) which can be visited after a climb up the
steep hill above the port. Excavations are being carried out at
the present time with some very rewarding results. Early
decorated pottery, flints, scrapers, hairpins, etc, as well as two
untouched graves (still with their complete skeletons and
some vases), were discovered 2 m down from the present
surface. There is also evidence of the use of fire on several
levels.

Returning across the island, if you take a road off to the right
just east of Blato, you can travel back on the old original route
which takes in the entire south side of the island. On this
coast there are many deep inlets of clear water, two or three
little fishing hamlets, one or two hotels — at Prižba and Brna

— and a splendid scenic drive which skirts sheer rocky heights on the one side and a glorious view of Lastovo and its archipelago of small islands on the other.

At the most easterly tip of Korčula island lies Lumbarda, first favoured by the ancient Greeks. Although only 6 km away from the city of Korčula, Lumbarda is completely different. Even the facial features of Lumbarda people can be detected. They are fairer than many Korčula people; they take life quietly and, in some indefinable way, they have an air about them of quiet satisfaction, perhaps emanating from the fact that they have been 'established' for at least 2,500 years. They are keen fishermen but their chief occupation has always been the production of their unique wine called *Grk*. This strong golden wine (15° if it is family-produced) is dry, almost bitter in taste. And some theorists say the word 'Grk' comes not from 'Greek', but from *gorki* meaning bitter. Be that as it may, drinking *Grk* is an experience seldom forgotten.

Lumbarda also has a 'corner' in sculptors, at least three of whom are well known internationally. One of them is Knez, a naïve sculptor whose work embodies simplicity and pathos in depicting country life and its burdens in the past, especially for peasant women.

There are one or two early chapels, but most holidaymakers love Lumbarda most for its fine shallow sandy beaches — three in all. There is one hotel and some attractive self-catering apartments built under trees by the sea.

From Lumbarda back to Korčula the prettiest way is by boat. Then one passes calm bays and the archipelago of Korčula's satellite islands, including Vrnik, famous for its stone quarrying, and Badija with its glorious monastery buildings. Just before reaching the quay below the city walls, Korcula's four post-war hotels are spread out on the port side. The first of these hotels was built in the early 1960s on the egg-box principle but, since then, architecture has changed and progressed, aided by strict rulings that the skyline must not be spoilt or interfered with. The original Hotel Park now looks very different. The second hotel, Marko Polo, has been planned so that, from the sea, its red roofs resemble those of an old Dalmatian village. The third hotel, Bon Repos, has been constructed round an existing pre-war building, taking advantage of the peaceful gardens planted with oleanders and olive trees that slope down to the bay. Among these trees there are also some excellent self-catering apartments. The fourth hotel, completed in 1985 is 'A' category with marble terraces, luxurious lounges, an attractively shaped outdoor swimming pool, and an *à la carte* taverna. But for me, the little hotel

Korčula on the promenade by the old loggia, completed in its *fin-de-siècle* style in 1910, is unique. In the 1980s it has been completely renovated, retaining its original red plush style. The pseudo-gothic stonework, and its marble terrace overlooking the *Riva*, are charming. And it is to this terrace that Korčula life is drawn of an evening: a quiet drink as you watch the sun go down; a greeting of friends, their children and grandchildren — this is the delightful warm essence of Korčula that never changes.

There is one other road on the island with a bus service. This leads west for 14 km, passing the hamlet of Kneža and finishing up at Račišće, an old-fishing port with a beautiful loggia and church, and one small hotel. In Račišće commodities often arrive in a van to be bought immediately from the driver and, when there is a catch of fish, it will be sold direct from the fishing smack to a crowd of housewives — the 'grapevine' telephone works well in island villages!

This can happen, too, in Korčula town itself, particularly in June and September, the two main tunny-fishing months. One sees the boat come in to the quay, and down one hurries with a large plastic bag to have one's fish weighed on the boat's scales, money handed over, and delicious fresh tunny or, even better, palamida — a small family relation — for lunch.

Korčula is a lovely island and its character, and that of its people, seem to appeal particularly to British visitors. Korčulans are transparently proud of their island and its heritage and are sure that there is no other to touch it for

The famous sword-pageant 'Moreška', performed only by people born in Korčula town

beauty and charm. Many believe that Marco Polo was not only imprisoned on the island but was also born there, and there are no documents to prove them wrong. Korčula has yet another unique heritage, the famous 'Moreška' sword-pageant and war-dance. This remarkable spectacle has now been performed in many parts of Europe, but only by Korčula men (and the one girl in the play) who must have been born within the precincts of Korčula town. Moreška, with its hair-raising clashes of cold steel, is something no visitor should miss when on this remarkable island.

MLJET

The island of Mljet stretches — long and narrow, hilly and darkly veiled — parallel with the Pelješac Peninsula towards Dubrovnik under whose protection it has remained since that republic's rise to power in the Middle Ages.

The island has a look of mystery about it when viewed from afar, whether seen from the mainland or the sea. There is often a mist round its heights and it always appears dark because of the trees that cover so much of it. From the sea it is impossible to distinguish any habitation. Life is all hidden behind the hills inland, and round the narrow-entranced bays on its shores.

Mljet is less than 100 sq km in area and mostly covered in forest under which wild cyclamen bloom in profusion in both spring and autumn, with the beautiful yellow chalices of the *sternbergia* joining the delicate mauve flowers in autumn. Much of the island is protected as a National Park and there is only one village bigger than a hamlet, well hidden in the centre and called Babino Polje. In the last two or three years the track to this village has been asphalted so that wheeled vehicles can now move about. There are four small ports on the northern coast which have deep water in well protected bays. Small ships of the Yugoslav shipping company, Jadrolinija, call at these harbours each day from Dubrovnik. During the summer there is also, since the road has been constructed on the island, a car-ferry to Polače from Trstenik, on Pelješac. Day excursions from Korčula also land visitors at Pomine at the western tip of Mljet: from here it is a short walk through the trees to the three beautiful lakes and the island monastery (now Hotel Melita) that most people come to see. Melita is the old name for Mljet.

People invariably seem to fall in love with Mljet, for it is one of the most endearing as well as beautiful islands. For years there was only the one small hotel, whose bedrooms are the former monks' cells. And there was no road, only donkey tracks. The monastery was founded in 1151 on the small inner island that lies in the middle of one of the seawater lakes — open to the sea by only the narrowest of shallow accesses. It was on the island of Mljet (Melita) and in this very difficult channel that St Paul was, in all probability, shipwrecked (Acts of the Apostles, Chapter 27).

A much earlier shipwreck, according to ancient legend, involved Ulysses. He, it says, found Calypso there and stayed on for seven years! No one, knowing Mljet, could blame him.

The south coast of the island is best visited by small boat — though not when a strong southerly is blowing. On this coast there is a Blue Grotto which can be entered at low tide in a flat-bottomed boat if the sea is calm, when the filtering light entering the cave bathes everything in an ethereal blue. Towards the eastern end of the island are two almost land-locked sandy bays, one of them cut off from the sea by a reef, except for the narrow gap that allows shallow craft to enter.

But it is at the western end of the island, at Pomine, that a new hotel has been built. Close to the transparent water of this beautiful bay with its protective islets, Hotel Odisej has wide terraces and restaurants just above the sea, but is only open during the summer months.

The next sizeable inlet, Polače, has few dwellings, but the huge walls of a Roman palace still rear up near the edge of the deep sound. In Roman times, rich patricians who were out of favour were exiled to Mljet. This huge pad was built, it is thought, by Agesilaus when he was banished by Septimus Severus. Later, according to some ancient writers, he and his son were pardoned by Caracalla when that emperor read the son's great poem, *Aleutica*.

The recently constructed road on the island means that cars can now land, and in some ways pollute, this idyllic place. But on my first visit there was only a footpath through the forests with, every now and then, sylvan clearings among the trees where the grapes and a few vegetables were grown. Even now, wandering along, one is likely to encounter a mongoose or two. These attractive small furry creatures were imported early in this century (as they were in Korčula) to rid the island of snakes, particularly adders. These vipers were *Boskoci*, an early form of serpent that hoops and stretches itself vertically in order to get away quickly when frightened. They are small and venomous, but so well has the mongoose colony done its work, that there are none left for it to hunt so it has been obliged to start on the eggs in farmyards, as well as the wild game on the island for its food.

The old medieval centre of Babino Polje is now very small, with a population of only a few hundred. It lies on a karst plain which is cultivated with vegetables, olives and grapes. The local people of Mljet make their own wine, some even in the old way — treading the grapes with their feet — which, they say, makes a better and purer wine.

Though it is possible for the people of Mljet to commute to Dubrovnik, the island retains its intense 'away-from-the-world' charm and it still seems unlikely — in spite of the new road and the cars — that this quality, almost a balm, will ever really change.

THE ELAPHITE ISLANDS

The last few islands of the Adriatic chain, The Elaphites, are scattered along the approach to Dubrovnik. Each of the larger ones — Šipan, Koločep, Lopud and, finally, Lokrum, are worth visiting for their medieval buildings — chapels, churches, towers — as well as for one or two well-known works of art. Šipan, Koločep and Lopud each have an hotel while Lokrum boasts the palace in which Maximilian, the ill-fated Emperor of Mexico and Hapsburg arch-duke, once lived. Šipan, Koločep and Lopud have fertile central valleys running from end to end which finish up in the sheltered bays — sandy in the case of Koločep and Lopud. The islands have always played satellite to Dubrovnik's star and, in the rich days of the Ragusan Republic, were used by Dubrovnik's patrician families as summer resorts. Beyond Dubrovnik, in the Bay of Župa on which Cavtat lies, there are one or two small islets which at one time were inhabited as leper colonies. But of those days only a wall or two remain. South of Cavtat the coast becomes unprotected and far less hospitable to small craft.

THE PELJEŠAC PENINSULA

Taking advantage of author's licence I am including Pelješac — so very nearly an island — in this section. The peninsula, from 1333 until this century, has remained under the jurisdiction of Dubrovnik producing salt and vegetables, wine, oil and cheese. There are a number of inland villages as well as some attractive hamlets and ports on both sides of this slim arm of land which is 65 km long. The inland valleys are very fertile and well enough endowed with natural water. They nestle between huge, and sometimes sheer, cliffs of rock — the strata often resembling some giant's efforts at building, so evenly has nature cleaved this stone. Vegetables, soft fruit — particularly peaches and nectarines — lemon and orange plantations, and vineyards are all intensively cultivated between the rocky heights while, on the lower slopes, pines and slim cypress trees, arbutus and many wild herbs and flowers – including the lovely blue *Iris dalmatinus* — grow in profusion. The women of the Pelješac villages are particularly good looking, with a fine carriage: they often still wear the full black or blue skirt, apron and headscarf of their national costume; and they still work hard in the fields and the vineyards.

The wines of Pelješac are extremely good, the most famous being *Dingač*, a very full-bodied dark red with a high (up to 17°) alcohol content. This wine is strictly controlled and grown in a restricted area on south-facing slopes near the sea. For centuries the growers had to take their grapes by donkey up over the steep mountain, walking from the vineyards that lay on the seaward slopes back to the depot where the grapes were fermented. Frequently, too hot a sun or a sudden late September shower of rain would ruin the fruit before it reached the factory. Only in the last five or six years has this been obviated by the tunnelling of a road through the mountain which emerges at the village of Potomje where a new, very modern wine factory has now been built. Much of the limited production of this excellent wine is now exported, but it fetches a good price in Yugoslavia, too. In President Tito's lifetime, a small reserve was kept for his enjoyment, a fact of which Pelješac is justly proud. There is a second wine, similar to *Dingač* but drier, which comes from some of the other south-facing slopes near by. This is *Postup*, not as heavy as *Dingač* and not as expensive and, for me, just as excellent to drink — particularly if one wants to stay awake in the afternoon!

There is no tourism in the interior of the peninsula, but along both shores there are villages, harbours and small hamlets where, though there may not be hotels, rooms in private houses can be found. Of these, Drače and Trpanj on the north-facing shore are the biggest. Trpanj was once an important harbour and there are sizeable reminders of Roman times there. Drače is smaller and open to the *Bura* wind, but has a substantial harbour arm for sheltering small boats and yachts.

On the southern shores of Pelješac — mostly sheer and with little protection from the southerly winds — there are one or two completely sheltered harbours. These are Trstenik and Žuljana. Žuljana is a delightful small place at the foot of a narrow tree-filled valley. There is fine sand edging its small bay, a restaurant, and some private rooms. The Romans, needless to say, found it first and left a few remains. Very recently, a road has been constructed linking Žuljana with the main road along the peninsula so that a donkey or small boat are no longer a necessity for getting there.

Trstenik, further west and opposite Polače on the island of Mljet, has a huge and magnificent harbour left from the days when ships called in to take *Dingač* directly on board. It is above Trstenik that the best *Dingač* is grown. These days Trstenik harbour is little used except by the car-ferry and a few tourist sailing-ships. There is a café there and a few private rooms to be let in the old houses. The harbour is excellent for yachts.

The main tourist centre on Pelješac is the old merchant navy port of Orebić, facing the walled city of Korčula less than a sea mile away. Orebić has a maritime history: the splendid stone houses bear witness to this. They were built by the old sea captains and ship owners close to the sea in lovely gardens, and they can be distinguished by their ornate dormer windows. Owning a sailing ship in past centuries, when communications were slow, meant constant anxiety until you could spot the craft through a telescope sailing safely to port. The top of the house was a vantage-point which gave a better visual trajectory. Facing south in such a warm climate, the gardens of these old houses were planted for shade with trees and palms, many flowers and beautiful stone columns and balustrades.

There are four main hotels built to one side of the port among big pine trees and cypresses along the sunny shore. The scent of these trees in summer is strong, and walking is extra pleasant. On the mountainside above Orebić, the peak of Sveti Ilija — St Elijah or, as the Italians called it, Monte Vipera — rears up, almost sheer, to its height of 961 m. Its lower slopes grow almonds, pomegranates, oranges and lemons as well as grapes and olives. But its upper slopes are almost bare, showing the white karst rock of which it is formed. A stiff walk up a path to its crest takes three to four hours, but the view of the Adriatic at dawn on a fine morning is memorable. It is said that on specially clear days the Italian coast can be seen a full 145 km away.

At the very tip of Pelješac, and sheltered by two long arms of low rocky land, is the fishing port of Lovište. Here life appears to be timeless, with the large tunny-fishing boats lazily stirring in the harbour waiting for their next sortie, and the villagers quietly mending nets, or seeing to the drying of the figs. These figs are a cottage industry; after picking, they are set over a sulphur fire to cleanse and preserve the fruit before it is threaded on a string with a bay leaf placed between each fig like a handsome edible necklace.

Lovište, until very recently, was completely cut off from the outer world except by donkey or boat. The post arrived by donkey along a rough stony track, having first passed the two small and nearly deserted villages up on the mountain, and a couple of Illyrian graves along the way. Now Lovište has been opened up by asphalt, the road threading its mountainous way from Orebić. But Lovište people still think of Korčula as quite a long way off (a journey of about eight sea miles!) and send affectionate messages to relatives, should one be passing that way.

There is a small hotel in the little port called Tamaris, a few private rooms to let, an autocamp, and a small self-service shop; though the stone table by the harbour still sells meat, fish, fruit and vegetables as they arrive by boat or van.

The post office, main café and restaurant share the same building. It is called 'Partižanska Veza' – the Partisans' Network – and is still a poignant reminder of how active the Partisans were along the entire peninsula. So active were they in fact, that Hitler gave his local commander specific orders to be extremely and particularly hard on these people and their families. New red roofs on the old houses along the entire length of Pelješac bear witness to the ruthless repression of those passionate defenders of country and freedom whose houses were systematically burnt as reprisals.

C·H·A·P·T·E·R· 3
Inland Yugoslavia

MACEDONIA

Only two of the six states that make up the Federal Republic of Yugoslavia have absolutely no seaboard: Serbia and Macedonia. And while Serbia does have a protected outlet to the Black Sea by way of the Danube, the modern Yugoslav state of Macedonia has no outlet at all.

Macedonia is the most easterly of the republics and borders on Bulgaria, Greece and Albania. Being of such an ancient culture, one can scarcely help clothing it in one's mind with an air of mystery. It has such dignity. Alexander the Great's father was Macedonian, though his red-haired mother, Olympias, may well have been Illyrian-Albanian. Kliment and Naum, disciples of Cyril and Methodius in Salonika, were Greek Macedonians who came to Lake Ohrid in the ninth century, continuing the work started by Cyril and Methodius of creating the Cyrillic alphabet, still used throughout Greece, Russia and Bulgaria, as well as in the eastern states of Yugoslavia–Serbia, Montenegro and Macedonia itself.

The country seems utterly timeless. The people are still cloaked with an old-world courtesy. The land, interspersed though it is with modern cities, seems quite biblical in time and custom with, on the rolling landscapes, shepherds and shepherdesses following their flocks, and men on Lake Dojran catching their fish with the aid of migrating birds, as they have done since time immemorial.

The Macedonians are a proud people, in spite of centuries of great hardship under the Turkish Empire. Theirs is a very old form of the Slav language of which they are proud, but it was not until the setting up of the modern Yugoslav state that they were allowed to use that language legally — in their parliament, in their official documents, and in their schools and universities.

Macedonia is a country of mountains and lakes: of old Macedonian balconied houses, of glorious early Orthodox monasteries, churches, and some mosques, many of which are still in use. Their crops include the famous Balkan tobacco, and *Papava somniferum*, the large and very beautiful poppy head from which opium and its derivatives are obtained. All the world heard of Skopje (see Chapter 5) when the earthquake struck in 1963, but not so many know that, on the outskirts of that city, there is one of the most up-to-date pharmaceutical factories in Europe. For 50 years it has been manufacturing the most sophisticated by-products of *Papava somniferum*. But Macedonia is very much an agricultural country still, with sheep that produce milk for some of the best natural yogurt and *kiselo mleko*, which resembles a little the French *crème fraîche*, but less soured.

Macedonia's history is extraordinarily complicated, parts of the country being dominated at various times by numerous outside powers, including Bulgaria, Serbia and Greece as well as, for 500 years, the Turks.

At the partition of the Roman Empire in AD 395 the whole of Macedonia became part of Byzantium. But at the end of the sixth century the Slavs began to arrive from the north, encroaching as far as the sea at Salonika so that, from this time, the Balkan people began to change ethnographically. A little later, at the end of the seventh century, the new country of Bulgaria, made up also of Slav tribes from the north, overran Macedonia, spreading for a while, during the tenth century, across the land which now constitutes Albania, almost to the shores of the Adriatic Sea. But by 1018, the western half of the land again came under Byzantine rule as a Greek province. There were further incursions by Bulgaria, but these were short-lived and Macedonia remained, by and large, under Byzantium until the fourteenth century.

It was during the periods of Byzantine rule that the country was endowed with some of the most lovely of the world's treasures. Byzantine architecture, frescoes and icons can be seen at their best in Macedonia. For, in spite of Turkey's Muslim efforts to destroy the churches and obliterate their works of art, many of the icons escaped destruction by being hidden, and some of the finest frescoes were preserved by the very plaster with which they were covered.

In the fourteenth century the strong Serbian Nemanja dynasty spread its influence south into Macedonia when Stefan Dušan had himself crowned in Skopje in 1346. He took the title of 'Emperor and Autocrat of the Serbs and Greeks, the Bulgarians and Albanians': a huge area of land to administer in those days of slow communication. But the Serbian Empire was not to last very long after Stefan Dušan's death in 1355. In 1389, at the Battle of Kosovo Polje, Serbian power was eliminated and the way was clear for the great Turkish Empire gradually to spread its tentacles across the whole of eastern Europe, and even to the banks of the Sava River at the very gates of Zagreb for a short period of time. Indeed, in 1529 and 1683 they encroached further still, almost to Vienna, but the Austro-Hungarian alliance was able to push the Turks back and, in the Treaty of Karlovci in 1699, the Ottoman Empire receded to the eastern borders of Croatia. But as far as Macedonia, Serbia, Bosnia and Montenegro were concerned this made no difference, and the Ottoman overlordship with its influence over dress, religion, eating habits and general way of life persisted until the end of the nineteenth century.

In all this time, the freer, happier, medieval days of brave exploits were never forgotten, kept alive by epic poems, ballads and folklore. When freedom at last returned, the Macedonians eagerly adopted once more the old traditions of their culture, and revelled in the fact that they could again speak publicly in their own language.

There are still many Albanians in Macedonia and a great number of them still wear oriental dress but, Muslim or Orthodox Christian, they are Macedonian first, and intensely proud, after so many centuries, to be once more a self-governing state.

Macedonia is mainly agricultural, and the countryside is varied and very attractive. The people of the villages still believe in the old herbal medicines and will provide you with the recipe — and even the requisites — for tisanes or poultices to cure any ill. There is an old saying, *Za sekoja balka ima bilka* — 'For every ill there is a herb'. Grannies will still give a drop of laudanum in water to a fretful child with toothache, but there is no drug problem in the country — perhaps because they are so accustomed to living side by side with the poppy fields. All the same, the growing of *Papava somniferum*, and the provision of the seed, as well as the harvest, is tightly controlled.

This poppy likes the same sort of climate and soil as the grape, and the wines they produce, including the dark red *Prokupac* — they call their red wines black — a white wine, Tikveš, and Joška found only near Lake Dojran, ease life along very pleasantly. Other occupations include the growing of cotton, and a large production of rice. This rice is excellent, especially for risotto: not so 'arid' as the long-grained varieties, and not so cloying as 'pudding' rice.

Macedonia has its share of mountains and lakes, the three largest lakes being Ohrid, Prespa and Dojran. All three are fairly close to each other in the south of the country and closely bordered by Greece and Albania. Of the three, Ohrid with its lovely and historic Orthodox monasteries and churches is the best known, while the other two — Prespa and Dojran — have yet to be discovered by the world at large.

The best-known mountains are the Šar Planina, where many Yugoslavs like to ski in winter. These mountains (near Tetovo and its famous 'painted' mosque) are well known both for the mountain sheep which produce high-quality wool and rich creamy delicate-flavoured milk, and for the Šar breed of dogs that protect the sheep. In fact, these splendid big animals protect their masters and families in the mountain villages as well. For they are wolf killers — no idle boast — as, on the unpeopled top heights of the Šar Mountains, the European wolf still lives in freedom. In a hard winter he will come down to the flocks of sheep and into the villages for food, but soon learns to respect his shaggy and faithful opponent.

Macedonia is a delightful and fascinating country, and still very much underdeveloped as far as tourism is concerned. It is a marvellous place to explore by car. There are two main arterial roads leading through Skopje (see Chapter 5) to the lakes which take in some attractive towns like Prilep (centre of the tobacco growing industry), Kavadarci (centre of the wine growing area), Štip and its spa, and Strumica near another spa whose waters arrive at 75° Centigrade! While not far from Titov Veles (a fascinating oriental town on the River Vardar) is Stobi, one of the most extensive archaeological sites from Roman and earlier times in Europe. Destroyed by an earthquake in AD 518, extensive excavations have already brought to light fine coloured mosaic flooring, as well as water and central heating ducts and the foundations of large houses. There is also beautiful stone tracery with carvings of birds and animals: enough to give more than a hint of just how luxurious life in eastern Europe was under Rome and Byzantium.

North of Štip, as well as several other notable monasteries

and churches such as Lesnovo, Nagovičano and others, there is the now quiet village of Kratovo. Gold and silver have always been mined near by and, in the sixteenth century, Suleiman II minted silver coins here. That mint still worked, well on into the next century.

GREATER SERBIA

The boundaries of Greater Serbia — with the federal capital Belgrade lying on the banks of the Sava and Danube rivers in its north-east corner —. extends to cover Vojvodina in the north, and Kosovo (Kosovo-Metohija) in the south. The former is the great fertile area of the Danube basin which supplies a large proportion of Yugoslavia's agricultural needs. The latter is squeezed between Montenegro, Albania and Macedonia, and has an Albanian ethnic majority who are sometimes known as Šiptari (from Sqiperia), though this is not a popular term among Kosovo people.

Although many Serbian and Macedonian families have lived for centuries in this area there has, in the last few years, been a bubble of nationalistic feeling on the part of this Albanian majority, which has burst into manifestations and demonstrations in its main cities Priština and Prizren — and in other centres such as Peć. Peć was the place in which, in 1346, the Serbian Orthodox Church created the patriarchate, the convent, library and churches of which are still in existence and working today. Yet there was recently arson even here, and some of the priceless books and documents in the library were destroyed.

It is sad that there should be strife in what is some of the most beautiful countryside it is possible to see. The Albanian majority could surely never wish to become part of the country of Albania, with all the restrictions this would entail. But some of them, and I have seen this voiced in an interview on Yugoslav television, would like the region to become a full-blown separate state, rather than an autonomous region of Serbia which it now is. A few of the hotter heads even dream of flying a separate flag!

For some families — all of them Muslim — Albanian is their first language; Turkish their second (for the Koran) and Serbo-Croat, the language in official use, coming a poor third. But what would happen if Kosovo did become a state within the Federation? For a start they would undoubtedly lose the enormous annual injection of money and technology that the rest of Yugoslavia has poured in to help them into a twentieth-century standard of life. This may be the century of national awakening but surely, with the installation of schools, universities and trade opportunities that have been provided by the richer areas for Kosovo since the war, reason and expediency must prevail in an area with so much potential to offer.

From a tourist point of view, the oriental life of the region is an enchanting sight; while the monasteries of the area and their treasures offer endless delight. The mountains and valleys are breathtaking with, perhaps, the exciting road over the Čakor Pass taking pride of place. It is near this pass, which leads to Peć, that the Rugovo Canyon has given rise to one of the most blood-curdling of medieval legends. Celebrated in dance, it tells of past deeds and feuds among families and tribes: of how no man of those families ever died in his bed; and how no girl dared cast eyes at a man on the enemy side. The dancers are dressed in white felted woollen cloth, with high boots. They jump high and menacing to the music which is solely a sinister sounding of the drums.

North of Kosovo the Serbian countryside becomes more gentle; in fact, some of the villages and farms among the smaller hills are reminiscent of the *bocage* country of French Normandy. It was in this area that the Serbian Kings of the Middle Ages did much of their fighting, and built many of their finest monasteries — including that of Studenica, which celebrated its eight hundredth anniversary in 1986.

The Drum Dance of Kosovo tells of past feuds and brave deeds

To the east and on one of the oldest trade routes to Istanbul, Persia and Central Asia, lies the town of Niš, close to the Morava River and its tributory, Nišava. Niš, the birthplace of the Emperor Constantine, boasts a spa; Mediana a remarkably well-preserved complex of villas with many mosaics and statues; and Cele Kula — The Tower of Skulls. During the first uprising on the part of the Serbs against the Ottoman occupation, the Turks built a tower, setting into it the skulls of dead Serbian soldiers. Altogether 952 heads were used for this grisly project, as if they were bricks. Preserved behind glass, what remains of this Tower of Skulls can still be seen today. It is about 2.5 km from the centre of Niš, on the road to Pirot. But what is so sad about the whole terrible episode is that documents show that the uprising was doomed to failure before it began. Because of the procrastination and overlong discussions on the part of the would-be liberators, the Turks got wind of it and were able to reinforce their troops. Had the Serbs been successful there would have been no Cele Kula to grieve over. The irony is that they may have got into the habit of procrastination from those very overlords they were trying to overthrow, whose lazier way of life had been superimposed on them for more than 400 years.

The main road to Belgrade continues through southern Serbia, passing some of the most interesting areas of this attractive and very rural part of the country, with its tiny villages and small farms. To the east of this artery, nestling among hills lighted up in autumn with the red and gold tints of the trees, is Sokobanja. This delightful spa, set on the slopes of steep hills, is a mixture of the very modern with the old world. It was known to the Romans, but there is now an extremely modern medical centre equipped with the latest diagnostic computerised machinery for all thoracic and pulmonary conditions. The large medical staff treat patients from all parts of Yugoslavia as well as those from the big mining industry of the area, and foreign visitors as well. But seeing the crowds of people in the vicinity of Sokobanja is not an indication of a country bound up in hypochondria or illness. There is an old saying: 'Sokobanja, Soko-grad, dodješ mator, odeš mlad' — 'Sokobanja, Soko-town, arrive elderly, depart young!' And for many Yugoslavs a visit to a spa is taken for pure pleasure. It is a holiday back in time to the gracious days of the nineteenth century and, though they may drink a glass of spa water for show, it is the hotel and social life they come to enjoy, much as English people visiting Malvern and Harrogate once sought.

The centre of Sokobanja is a wide tree-lined boulevard with

a park to one side. There are cafés with terrace tables under the trees, and the soothing sight of water and fountains is never far away. The flower beds are formal with clipped box hedges; there is no wheeled traffic near the promenade, and an attractive air of pink champagne — almost Parisian 'froth'!

The main treatment centres are above the town near the hotels. Foreign nationals can book in to the hotels, take in their treatment at the medical centre, have full board plus three excursions to places of interest during their stay for an all-in price of about 34 dollars (around £20) a day. But for the healthy, the hilly walks to waterfalls, fishing in the Moravica River for trout, or visiting the small ethnic museum which is housed in an ancient Serbian dwelling at the end of the promenade, and exploring the original 'Kursaal' is enough. Though a visit to Zaječar, and its glass factory is almost a 'must'. Part of its success lies, I think, in the imaginative ideas it has for its glassware. It is possible to buy this very good quality glass direct from the factory showroom at very reasonable prices.

Close to Zaječar there is a turning off the main road to Gamzigrad. Using small cart tracks skirting farm fields, and zig-zagging among the hay, maize and other crops, one suddenly comes upon the huge and very well preserved entrance gates of a Roman fortress. Gamzigrad dates back to the third and fourth centuries, and excavation is still going on over the very large area that the Roman garrison town covered. There are acres of foundations, mosaics, the walls of private houses, thermai, etc., and, for anyone attracted to the past, the remarkable sophistication of Roman life in a garrison town is there to see. The fortress defended the trade routes from Europe to the Middle East and Asia.

On the other side of the main road that leads north to Belgrade, and at about the same latitude as Gamzigrad, are the towns known as the three 'Ks' — Kruševac, Kraljevo and Kragujevac. Roughly within this triangle are some of the most beautiful Serbian monasteries, built at the zenith of Byzantine ecclesiastical building. Some are peopled by monks; others by nuns. For, whichever the sex, they are called monasteries — *manastiri* or, in Croatia, *samostani*.

Kruševac, at the time of King Lazar — he was killed at Kosovo Polje in 1389, and was the husband of Queen Milica — was the capital city of Serbia. Later, for a long period, it was the seat of a Pasha. It is still a thriving busy town with a very large, very modern hotel and a good deal of industry. On a hill at its centre are the remains of a fortified palace, and the church of Lazarica with its beautiful façades and portals.

Sadly, the frescoes were destroyed during the Turkish occupation, but the church, built by King Lazar — or Prince Lazar in this area of Serbia — in about 1375, still stands. It is an important example of one of the earliest structures of the Morava School. Its façades are of red and white brick and stone, and the delicate patterning of arches and rosettes are remarkable. It served as a model for many later churches, with its trefoil ground-plan. King Lazar ruled for 18 years and instigated many religious foundations during that time. He is still looked on as a hero, and is remembered in several ways, not only for his defence of Serbia and his beautiful churches. There is a dark red wine named after him, too. It is called Czar Lazar and is similar to the wine called after his beautiful queen, Milica. Both wines carry portraits of this famous and benign couple on their labels, portraits that can also be seen in the frescoes of some of the churches.

This is a very rich part of Serbia gastronomically, where the chefs seem to have retained the best of traditional Serbian foods together with the nicest additions from the long Ottoman occupation. Every menu will include *kajmak* — the famous Serbian cream cheese which is literally reamed cream, very much like Cornish cream, kept for a few days with a fresh layer added each morning. It will be served with *hors d'oeuvres*, or with cooked and skinned long red sweet peppers, or hot with rolls of charcoal-grilled minced and spiced meat, or as an accompaniment to grilled fillet steak. Then there will be fish, probably river trout; grilled pork; spit-roast lamb, in season; plaited and grilled long strips of veal; and spiced sausages. Salads are colourful, especially the delicious *Šopska Salata* which contains sweet peppers, cucumber, slivers of fiery capsicum and tomatoes, with a grated white cheese on top, dressed with wine vinegar and olive oil. Desserts include *baklava* and other cakes and pastries; *Kompot* which looks like stewed fruit, but seems to taste better; and *palačinke* (pancakes) stuffed with ground walnuts in an egg sauce. The ubiquitous Turkish coffee is almost essential after a meal such as this. Kruševac has a number of restaurants but, in the down-to-earth style of this ancient town, one of the most popular is the restaurant Rubin 'Vinjak 5' on the outskirts and at the end of a cul-de-sac. The entrance is nothing to look at — more like a booth at the back of a sports stadium — but inside are the gastronomic delights suitable for its name. *Vinjak* is cognac, and Rubin is a firm producing one of the best in Yugoslavia.

Because the inhabitants of Serbian Orthodox monasteries are so friendly and practical in their views on life, it is quite in order to have a good lunch before knocking on their doors! On the scenically attractive road between Kruševac and Kraljevo is the turning to Ljubostinija, a lovely and peaceful place.

The name of this large convent really translates as 'Love on the Rocks' — from *Ljubav* and *Stijena* — and an old legend says that it was near this beautiful area of hills and narrow valleys that King Lazar and Queen Milica first met. They are said to have fallen in love at first sight on a rocky outcrop.

Though there is no authentication for this story, it is a fact that Queen Milica, after the terrible outcome of the Battle of Kosovo Polje, founded the convent of Ljubostinija in 1395, taking in with her 300 other well-born women who were also widowed by the battle. Queen Milica became *Igumanija*, or prioress, taking the name of Eugenia, until she died in 1405. When her husband was killed, she managed to take the royal treasure with her to Ljubostinija, including his crown, which she hid in a small niche in the wall of the church, its wooden door concealed by an icon. It wasn't until the seventeenth-century that the Turks, who damaged the frescoes, actually found the cupboard, carrying away all the treasure. It has only recently been discovered that King Lazar's crown is still in Istanbul — on show in the Topkapi Palace! When I told the little nun who was guiding me round that I had actually seen the crown there, her face became quite transfigured with joy.

There is a second true story attached to that six-hundred year-old crown. When Peter Karadjordjević came to the throne of Serbia in 1903, he wanted to use the same crown and, believing it still to be in Ljubostinija, he had Queen Milica's

Czar Lazar and his queen Milica, immortalised on monastery walls and on wine labels

coffin opened. This was not only an act of great insensitivity, but it ruined the outer decoration of her tomb. And it was all for nothing. Milica's bones were inside the sarcophagus, but there was no crown. The queen's coffin can be seen today by the door inside the church, and that of her great friend Euphemia, a poetess, on the other side. Some of Euphemia's poems, telling of those troubled times at the end of the fourteenth century, are very moving.

Among the frescoes in the church is one showing the king and queen together. Another fresco portrays their sons, Stefan and Vuk, who were also killed at Kosovo Polje. Poor Milica! It was the arms of those sons that she gathered up after the battle of Kosovo to make an eternal lamp. Dečani was built earlier in the fourteenth-century by a former Stefan and Dušan, who reigned between 1331 and 1355.

There are today 50 nuns living at Ljubostinija, but they certainly don't spend all their time on their knees. Between them they tend the fields, shepherd the sheep, look after the bees, make the wine which they sell, produce embroidery, lace, basket-work — including arm-chairs — paintings, and a large garden full of flowers. On arrival we were taken to the parlour to be welcomed with Turkish coffee and *nešto slatko* — 'something sweet' — an almost obligatory and most Serbian custom.

Nešto slatko is served with protocol on a small tray on which are placed a dish of sugar-preserved fruit or a kind of very stiff jam, a glass with water in it, and some small spoons in a third dish. Never refusing, one takes a spoon, digs in to a little jam or a piece of fruit, eats it showing pleasure, and finally places the used spoon in the glass of water. The making of *nešto slatko* is a culinary art undertaken by all mothers and grandmothers in Serbia — and by nuns in their convents! It entails boiling a syrup until thick, cooking the fruit (which can be anything from quinces to raspberries), and then pouring the mixture on to a cold slab, so that it can be cut into squares when cold.

The nuns at Ljubostinija are very industrious and work an extremely long day. The old original bedroom cells above the wine cellars are still in use, but the beautiful church of creamy stone with rich decoration on its arches and windows is the centre of their life and happiness.

Žiča, another Orthodox monastery inhabited by nuns, is close to Kraljevo, and set on a plain near the entrance to the gorge cut by the River Ibar. It was built between 1208 and 1220 by Stefan Prvovenčani (Stefan the First-Crowned); all previous rulers were princes or župans. He ruled from 1217 to 1227.

Žiča, one of the earliest of the monasteries, is red in colour. It was the seat of the first autonomous Serbian bishopric, and it belongs to the Raška school of ecclesiastic Orthodox architecture, borrowing from the Romanesque. But, remembering its relationship with Mount Athos — the spiritual parent of the Orthodox Church — Žiča was, and still is, painted red. A few frescoes of the thirteeth-century and some especially beautiful examples of fourteenth-century work remain on the inside walls of the church; but what is really fascinating is that there are seven doorways in this quite small church. It was at Žiča, over a period of almost 200 years, that seven kings of the Nemanja dynasty were crowned and, for each new king, another doorway was created so that they could emerge as king where no one had ever stepped before.

Within the church there is a small and very intricate inlayed ivory and walnut coffin. It was made as a receptacle for the bones of Sv Sava — he who was the youngest son of Stefan Nemanija. He became a monk at Mount Athos, taking the name of Sava, and in 1219 became archbishop of the Serbian church. The name of Sv Sava still stands for education and emancipation in Serbian history. It was he who created the Serbian Orthodox Church, separating it from Greece and the archbishopric of Ohrid in Macedonia. Sv Sava's bones are not in that coffin at Žiča, for the Turkish overlords took them to Belgrade and burnt them as an example. Now, in Belgrade, a church is being built on the very spot at which the burning took place. This church had its third ceremony of consecration in 1984 and is being built by money given by the people, not all of them religious. But Sv Sava, and all he stood for, was an irreplaceable factor in Serbian destiny.

Close to Kraljevo (the second of the three 'Ks') there is another delightful spa called Vrnačka Banja. This spa has three springs of natural curative water — one warm at body temperature — and two cold. The clinic treats gastro-intestinal, liver and pancreas conditions, renal diseases, and metabolic disorders. Closely resembling Sokobanja, there are hotels flanking one side of its pedestrians-only promenade which makes it an easy and pleasant overnight stopping-place. The promenade is broad, with the park on its further side and, at one point, the paving is made up of black-and-white chequered squares. There are enormous chessmen available which the enthusiasts move about with great aplomb. Chess is a national game in Yugoslavia.

Lining the promenade are old-fashioned cafés and kiosks, while beyond the hotels at the end of the promenade is the town centre. If you walk past the post office, you come upon a very large open-air market. This is well worth a visit. There is special oven-ware pottery for baking local meat specialities; small wooden 'churns' for *kajmak*; leather wear; song birds; silks and woollens; *kajmak* itself; fruit, vegetables and meat; plates, dishes, glass and cheap jewellery — a mecca for souvenir-hunting.

You can wander in the park, or take a ride to the top of the

Detail of fresco. St Elijah, Morača Monastery

hill in the toy train. You can eat cream cakes and listen to the birds. You can visit monasteries, or the fortress of Maglič, built above the River Ibar in the thirteenth-century to defend those monasteries. Like Sokobanja, Vrnačka Banja is a light-hearted place and, whether it is the air or the potent mineral water, the whole seems to spell out 'Živeli' — 'Long Life' — the national toast of Yugoslavia.

Close to Kraljevo there is yet another monastery which really should not be missed. This is one of the oldest of all — Studenica — which celebrated its 800th anniversary in 1986 and has recently been designated by Unesco as one of the world's cultural treasures. It was founded by Stefan Nemanja and has always been closely associated with the convent of Žiča. Its name comes from the clear cool stream that runs near it. Influenced by his son, Sava, Stefan entered the monastery towards the end of his life, taking the name of Simeon, and then retiring to Chilandar monastery on Mount Athos where he died. Later, he was canonised as St Simeon Myrobliptos; his feast day is 26 February.

This lovely monastery of Studenica which had, in all, thirteen churches built within its precincts, is completely encircled by a wall against which are built the living quarters, the bell tower, two refectories, and the gate house. The main church, of the Virgin Mary, and the 'King's' church —

Studenica monastery celebrated its eight-hundredth year in 1986

dedicated to Saint Joachim and Saint Anne — are still in use, and a third church, Sv Nikola, has been excavated. The foundations of the ten other churches — still revered — have been brought into the overall plan of the beautiful gardens. Full of roses, phlox, petunias and groups of shady trees, it all makes an unforgettable picture.

There are ten monks living at Studenica and they happily talk to visitors and show them round their historic home. The frescoes in the churches are remarkable and among the most famous in the world. They reveal a new thirteenth-century style of Serbian Orthodox art, and are much less stylised than the early Greek examples. One very interesting feature of these Studenica frescoes is that, for the first time, the shoulders and arms of some of the female figures are shown bare and undraped. Another surprising feature is visible in the fresco depicting the Last Supper — *Tajna Večera* — which shows an extraordinary depth of perspective. In it, Christ is revealed not in the middle of the disciples, but sitting in the foreground on the left-hand side of the semi-circle of followers and, though they are eating from a bowl with their fingers, the table is laid with elegant knives.

Among the exhibits in the small treasury is the ring of King Stefan the First-Crowned, a heavily decorated gold filigree affair.

The monks work hard to augment their income by selling attractive souvenirs. These are imaginative — plates to hang on a wall handpainted with a picture of the monastery, table candles, 'monastery' T-shirts, and even carrier bags printed all over with some of the most famous frescoes. They are bought by visitors from all parts of the world, and when I was there in 1986 — the octocentenary — there was a family of Yugoslav origin who had all come all the way from Brisbane, Australia. It is estimated that 150,000 people visited Studenica during the six-month celebration of the anniversary, and the authorities built a new wide road to accommodate the enormous influx of coaches, buses and cars. Though the brothers live in such a secluded place, they are surprisingly interested in the outside world, and quick to make quite up-to-date and 'current-affairs' jokes. And they are not above sharing a glass or two of their excellent home-distilled *Šljivovica* with friends in their spick-and-span parlour.

Because there is so much to see in this famous monastery, it is good to know that there is a motel very close to Studenica with an open-air terrace to the restaurant overlooking the beautiful valley.

Kragujevac, the third of the three 'Ks', is now a modern

industrial city where, among other commodities, the Yugoslav version of the Fiat car — the Zastava — is manufactured. The present car factory occupies the sight of the nineteenth-century cannon and shot foundry, with its tall tower still in place. Kragujevac has always been a centre for the rich farming area surrounding it but, even 40 years on, for anyone who knows Kragujevac at all, it is the tragically poignant Šumarice Memorial Park on the outskirts of the town that comes first to mind. This monument marks for posterity one of the cruellest acts of the last war. It was here, in October 1941, that a whole age-group of children were taken with their teachers by the German troops occupying the area, and made to dig a long deep trench. Then, not knowing why, they were

One of Yugoslavia's most poignant memorials, in memory of all those children in class V

ordered to stand in a line in front of that trench to be shot, so that their bodies fell back into the grave they had been compelled to dig. This was a reprisal and warning to the Partisans. It will never be forgotten.

On the east of the main highway to Belgrade, and a little east of Kragujevac, is Despotovac — an intimidating name until one remembers the original meaning of 'despot'! This small town has now become a tourist centre, owing its fame partly to the very interesting and very extensive caves called *Resavska Pečina* and to the only early monastery to have a fortress of huge walls and towers built round it for protection against the Turkish invaders. Manasija (also known as Resava) was built by Despot Stefan between 1407 and 1418, near the Resava River which runs into the Morava. The architecture, known as the Morava School, is evident at Manasija just as it is at Ljubostinija, Lazarica and other churches. But Manasija is the only one in which marble was used exclusively in its construction. Thinking back, it is easy to understand why this and other religious centres were placed in such narrow hidden valleys, after the Ottoman Empire's arrival in the Balkans. Monks and nuns must have lived in constant fear.

Manasija's fortifications include eleven massive defence towers, and the surrounding walls are several metres thick. When I called in again in 1986 there were workmen aloft repairing the tops of the defences. It might seem anachronistic until you remember that the Yugoslav authorities have an obligation to keep historic buildings in good repair. A second point is that, together with agriculture, tourism is now the top priority for earning hard currency. But all that passes the nuns of Manasija by. They welcome visitors, but are most concerned with their quieter duties, and the dedication of their lives to their church, tending this lovely place and its spick-and-span rose gardens with quiet joy.

Further east in this part of Serbia the River Dunav (Danube) forms the border between Yugoslavia and Romania. On and near the great river there are some interesting places to visit. Apart from medieval fortresses such as Golubac (fourteenth-century and well preserved), there is the Iron Gates gorge with its famous marble plaque, carved in AD 103, known as Trajan's Tablet. This can still be seen high up on the walls of rock above the gorge. It was placed there when the Roman Emperor Trajan finished the road begun by Tiberius which was cut into the vertical face of the rock above the gorge. Excursion boats from Belgrade go slowly past the Tablet so that it is possible to photograph it, though not to reach it.

Quite close, and a little to the east of Trajan's Tablet, is the twentieth-century Djerdap Bridge across the Danube to Romania, with the huge hydro-electric power station built as a joint project by the two countries. It is possible to visit the power station, which is a remarkable feat of engineering. From the Yugoslav side, and not far away, the first Roman attempt to bridge this mighty river is visible.

Following the river upstream, one comes to Donji Milano-vac, a village with a very nice modern hotel, and a splendid view of Romania across the river. A stay of two or three days here is well worth while for there is much to see. To begin with there is 'gold in them there hills' just inland from the Danube. This gold, mined in Roman times, is still quarried at Majdanpek along with copper. It was extensively worked by the Turks — Majdan meaning quarry — and comes from the quartz of the Homolje Mountain. As well as the official mining activities, the villagers have long had a bonus pastime. The gold flakes off the mountain to be brought down by the rains into the River Pek, and panning for gold regularly puts gilt on the gingerbread for the local inhabitants. Now the enterprising tourist agents in the area are sharing the gold with tourists. They arrange excursions to include river-side barbecues, gold-panning and folklore performances, plus a visit to the spectacular Ceremosnja Caves and their stalactites and stalagmites. The small town of Kučevo is the centre of this enterprising offer. There is a new hotel, some souvenir shops

The castle of Golubac, one of many still standing on the banks of the Dunav River

110

and, apart from gold dredged up which tourists can keep (if any!), souvenirs include pieces of carved onyx, also found nearby.

The River Pek, with its gold, runs into the Dunav, and this all fits in with the legend of Jason and the Golden Fleece. It seems likely that Jason sailed up the Dunav when he heard about the Fleece. It is an ancient custom in this area to anchor a sheep's fleece in the river and wait for the specks of gold to collect in the fine mesh of the wool.

Just north of Majdanpek, on the shores of the Dunav near Donji Milanovac, is one of the most remarkable archaeo-logical discoveries in Europe — the 8,000-year-old settlement of Lepenski Vir. It is estimated that there were about 600 inhabitants in this ancient river-bank community. They knew how to make and use fire; their dwellings were probably triangular both vertically and in the ground plan; and in some cases their hearthstones are still visible. When the existence of this settlement became known in 1967 it had world-wide archaeological repercussions as it formed a new bridge between modern and Paleolithic man. A total of 136 dwellings were discovered, all built between 6,500 and 5,500 BC.

It is thought that towards the end of the Ice Age — around 20,000 BC — an early Stone Age European community inhabited the caves on the banks of the Dunav in the Iron Gates gorge, sheltering in them until about 7,000 BC when the climate became warmer. This change in temperature and climatic condition made it possible from that time to live on open ground. And they began to spread out into small communities, choosing areas of land rich in wood for fuel, game, edible fruit and water. The name *Vir* means whirlpool, and it is possible that the Lepenski inhabitants chose the site because they lived partly on fish which abound, and are easier to catch, in the eddies of these pools.

It seems that they were a complex and well-organised community with many cults and funeral rites. Graves within the village of dwellings, some near the hearths, were accorded to only a few members of each generation. Children came in for special treatment, too, being buried invariably at the rear end of the dwellings underneath the floor. The everyday tools and implements found at Lepenski Vir are of remarkable quality and include fish-hooks, clubs, knives, awls and chisels. Then there are pestles, balls and polishers. But perhaps the most remarkable of all are the sculptures, both abstract and of recognisable figures. These are sculpted on huge stone boulders, the eyes and nose clear to see and the mouth almost fish-like, while in some examples there are symbolic hands, or a pattern looking almost like fish-scales underneath the face. Some people consider the faces fish-like, too; some fish-man deity, perhaps. But, if you go to Donji Milanovac — the nearest riverside village — it is noticeable that the inhabitants tend to have just the same strong features as those carved in stone about 8,000 years ago — the same wide lips and prominent sloping eyebrows.

There is also evidence that, as the community progressed, its members became stockmen and farmers, domesticating some animals and improving the stock. They also started to cultivate some strains of wild wheat, as is clear from excavations of the later period. A visit to Lepenski Vir is a remarkable and strangely moving experience.

On the northern side of Belgrade is Novi Sad, capital city of the autonomous region of Vojvodina, the largest and most prolific agricultural area of Yugoslavia. Here the fields resemble prairies, and there seem to be great forests of maize.

One of many remarkable finds at Lepenski Vir dating from about 6,000 BC — a household god?

Not only is the maize used to flavour and make bread and feed fowl but, in the older and more rural communities, the husks — mixed in with wool and renewed each year — have long been considered superior to springs in mattresses. Apart from the corn, there are hectare after hectare of sweet peppers, tomatoes, wheat and fruit orchards, farmed with up-to-date technology and giant machinery. So important is it to Yugoslavia to be as self-supporting as possible, that news broadcasts throughout the country include progress of the crops at harvest time.

There are three main roads to Novi Sad from Belgrade, but the longest route, via Ruma, is well worth the detour. Ruma has a local market near the centre of the town where the colour of the produce — reds, greens, yellows, mauves — is like an Impressionist painting, and the prices are less than anywhere else in the country. There are pottery stalls with cooking utensils, dishes and bowls, and great water jugs like those taken to the fields by the farmers.

So many minorities live in Vojvodina on both banks of the River Dunav that the Novi Sad parliament is conducted in no less than five different languages. The centre of the town is attractive and has an old-world air about it. There is a strong Austro-Hungarian influence to the architecture as it was an outpost of Empire in the days of Ottoman rule in eastern Europe.

The city lies with the Dunav bordering it on one side and the foothills of Fruška Gora on the other. Fruška Gora is famous for the vineyards on its slopes, and especially for a sparkling wine called *Fruškogorski Biser*. The town itself began as a small merchant and fishermen's village created by craftsmen, shopkeepers and others attracted to the trade brought by the garrison and its ancillaries living at the huge fortress of Petrovaradin. It wasn't until 1748 that Novi Sad was granted the status of a royal free town administered by local dignitaries instead of military jurisdiction. By the beginning of the nineteenth-century several schools of varying Christian denominations had been built, and there were Orthodox, Roman Catholic and Jewish hospitals. But the town suffered in 1848 — the year of revolutions — when it was bombarded, set on fire and looted by a Hungarian garrison stationed in the fortress. Today it is a quiet and business-like city of ethnic minorities which include, as well as Serbs, Romanians, Hungarians, Slovaks, Ruthenians and Ukrainians.

From a sightseeing point of view the massive fortress of Petravaradin is almost overwhelming. Built in 1694, it is still completely preserved. Its completion took 88 years and it was modelled on the system evolved by Vauban, that old master of French fortification. It lies strategically on a bend of the river where there had been fortifications even in the time of the Romans. There are high walls rearing up from the river, wide dykes which could be mined in case of invasion, and a whole network of underground corridors on four levels, in all, 16 km long. A tremendous bastion between the Austro-Hungarian Empire and that of the Turkish invaders, the Hapsburg monarchy regarded it as 'The Gibraltar of the Danube'. Today all is peaceful in the grounds and passages of the great fortress which is among the largest in Europe. The officers' mess is now a high-class restaurant. There is a museum and a guide service, and an hotel often used by shooting parties, as game is abundant on the hills of Fruška Gora. The old buildings have a strange beauty of their own, and the views across the great river are lovely.

Beyond Novi Sad the entire area of Vojvodina, set in the flat lands of the Pannonian Plain, becomes very rural, punctuated with small villages in which one or another minority pre-dominates: it is sometimes possible to distinguish which by the architecture of the village church. Or perhaps there will be a wedding taking place, or a christening. At such times the national dress worn will give a clear indication, whether it is a Slovak, Hungarian, Romanian or even old-style Russian affair. Another interesting phenomenon in this area is the number of Yugoslav naïve painters these tiny communities have pro-duced. These painters have become famous in the art world far beyond the frontiers of their own adopted country. They still live in their village cottages and tend their animals and farms, painting in their spare time. And it is possible sometimes to call at their homes where their wives will show you some of their work. One of the best known of these painters of Primitives is Martin Jonas who lives in the village of Kovačica where most of the population is of Romanian extraction. His pictures are delightful and fetch a good price but, entering his home, it is quite evident that he still prefers the simple life of his village.

BOSNIA

Due south of Vojvodina is inland Bosnia, a country of mountains, lakes, hills, valleys and woodland. Crossed by rivers, there are ancient towns, castles and many famous landmarks. Here the Turkish Empire ruled supreme for around 500 years, and some of the old places under Turkish rule have been immortalised in famous books such as *Travnik Chroni-*

cles and *Bridge over the Drina*, both written by the Nobel Prize winner, Ivo Andrić.

In the last 35 years life in Bosnia/Hercegovina has changed dramatically. Until the end of the last war the people, generally, were underprivileged and backward in a worldly sense, the great natural resources of their country almost untapped. Today they are a forward-looking twentieth-century people with tremendous potential: a bustling commercially-oriented community superseding the old slow-as-you-please agricultural way of life near the towns. But there is a vast area where tiny villages perch on the slopes of hilly country and many of the people still like to wear oriental dress. They still use the old traditional metal dishes and water jugs of their forefathers and cook Turkish-style food on charcoal as often as they use their new-fangled electric stoves, though television has reached nearly all their homes and there is electricity for every dwelling.

The rest of Yugoslavia is still inclined to look on Bosnia with a kind of amused and affectionate tolerance, ignoring the fact of their modern success and, indeed, the perspicacity of their merchants throughout the ages. Yugoslav jokes often make a Bosnian character the fall-guy — much as the country Irish are often the butt in the UK or Midwest farmers in the USA. Be that as it may, the average Bosnian is a shrewd character in real life, just as their kings were highly successful until the final débâcle when the Turks vanquished first the Serbs to the east in 1389, and then spread out over most of Bosnia in 1463. Many Bosnians fled to the Adriatic coast and its islands at that time, some going as far as Klis, above Split, and even Senj where they formed the nucleus of the famous Uskok pirate-heroes: *Uskok* coming from the Serbo-Croat word for refugee.

Of the Bosnians who stayed on under the Turks, a number were Bogomil heretics who had previously held out for hundreds of years in Bosnia against the Roman Catholic religion. In some ways the Bogomil beliefs were more akin to Islam than to Rome. And it is a fact that these Bogomils fared quite well under the Turks, many of them preferring to become Muslim rather than be subject to the Pope. By turning to Islam they were allowed to keep their lands and posses-sions so that, often, those in control of the new Turkish Bosnia were actually Slav by birth and of aristocratic lineage, yet Muslim in faith.

The 'Vali' or Pasha bothered little about local affairs though his seat was in Bosnia — first at Sarajevo, then at Banja Luka, and thirdly at Jajce — and the Bogomil noblemen continued to administer as they had always done, though now as Bosnian *Begs* or *Beys*. At the same time Orthodox and Roman Catholic Christians were not persecuted, though they were precluded from holding official power.

In the twentieth century what most people know about the Bogomil religion is confined to a knowledge of their enormous tombstones with their strange carved signs and figures and their curious, often asymmetrical, shape.

The Bogomil religion rejected the Old Testament, the Incarnation, the Cross, and the Sacrament. They believed that man must spend his entire life striving after asceticism, and that the material world was created by Satan, the dark angel Lucifer.

In the words of an anonymous writer of the twelfth-century:

> He took mud from the earth and from it He moulded Man
> in his own image.
> And then He commanded the second angel to enter into the
> body of mud,
> And He took from it a particle and from it
> He made another body in the shape of a Woman.
> Then He commanded the angel of the first heaven to enter
> into it.
> The angels greatly wept when they learned that they had
> mortal bodies
> And that they differed in form one from another.
> Finally He made them perform the act of carnal love with
> their bodies of clay,
> Without their knowing that they were committing a sin . . .

There are many Bogomil tombs in Bosnia and Hercegovina and some of the easiest to see are at Radimlja, near Stolac, where there is a necropolis containing 133 tombstones. Near Stolac, too, there are the ruins of a third-century BC castle, built with huge 'Cyclopean' stones.

Apart from the capital city of Bosnia, Sarajevo (see Chapter 5), Banja Luka, on the River Vrbas is one of Bosnia's most important towns as, indeed, it was in the Middle Ages and in Roman times when it was a *castrum*. It was also, through the centuries, a centre of resistance — against the Turks, against the Austro-Hungarian occupation and, in the last war, one of the earliest against the German occupation. But, curiously, some of the most lovely remains from those past centuries were endowed by Bosnians who courted the Ottoman Empire, embracing the Muslim faith. For example, Beglar-Bey built the mosque of Ferhad Pasha in 1583, an extraordinarily beautiful monument to Islam, lavishly decorated inside, and with some superb oriental graves in the yard outside — one of them that of Ferhad Pasha himself. Another is the tomb of a vizier, Ali-Pasha Rizvanbegović, whose name could hardly be more Slav! The Arnaudija mosque was built nearby in 1587 by a man of Albanian extraction, Hassan-Effendi, who became treasurer of Bosnia.

Due south of Banja Luka on the road to Mostar is Jajce, on the banks of the Pliva and Vrbas Rivers, one of the most photogenic old towns in Bosnia. Its centre is almost a museum of oriental Bosnian life in past centuries. It is built on a steep hill with magnificent waterfalls below it. The hill is egg-shaped — which probably accounts for the town's name, Little Egg, or *Jajce* — and there are substantial remains of the medieval citadel and its surrounding walls. The castle was built by the Croat duke Hrvoje Vukčić-Hrvatinić early in the fifteenth century — a reminder of how closely associated Croatia and Bosnia have always been.

The huge gravestones with strange carved figures are all that is left of the Bogomil heretic religion

In this old part of the town there is an altar to Mithras in the remains of a temple. There are the catacombs and vaulted tombs built by Duke Hrvoje Vukčić. There is a mosque, and some well-preserved Bosnian/Turkish houses, and there are the gateways into the old city — the Banja Luka, the Travnik and the Bosnia Gates. According to legend, the remains of the last Bosnian king, Stjepan Tomašević, murdered by the Turks in 1463, still lie in the Franciscan monastery at Jajce. Almost 500 years after the death of the king, the foundations of the Socialist Republic of Yugoslavia were established in Jajce in 1943. Tito was in Jajce at that time and the old catacombs were used by the council as a secure place for planning meetings and for radio contact with the Partisans.

The dramatic waterfalls at Jajce are in the heart of the town

There are modern hotels, including one perched above the beautiful Plivska Lakes about 1 km away from the town centre. The lakes, surrounded by trees, are a lovely sight and the old watermills, tiny little wooden-roofed structures, are still in place. These days the lakes are a well-known canoe and kayak rendezvous.

Not far away from Jajce is Travnik, known to the world from Ivo Andrić's book *Travnik Chronicles*. The first records of this town date from the year the last Bosnian king died, but it is now known that there were Celts, as well as Illyrians and Romans, who came here to pan for gold. For nearly 200 years during the reign of the Ottoman Empire it became the seat of the Turkish Viziers and there still seems to be in this old town an atmosphere left over from those times: a curiously strong feeling of no hurry, tomorrow will do. There is a wealth of Turkish-style houses and, in the very centre of the town, a large and very beautiful decorated mausoleum around which washes the traffic of modern life — cars, buses, and many bicycles. The mosque of Sulemanija is fascinating. Its ground floor allows room for shops, while above there is the mosque proper, richly decorated.

Think of Višegrad and, once you have been there, you think of the bridge over its wide river, the Drina. Low, and with eleven arches, the bridge is 175 m long and is a lovely sight. The town of Višegrad lies on the road between Bosnia and Istanbul and for this reason was an important link in the Turkish lines of communication. Records go back to 1433, but it was the powerful Bosnian overlord, Mekmet-Pasha Sokolović, born of Slav ancestry in this area, who built the bridge as a tribute to his place of birth. He could afford to, being Grand Vizier to no less than three Sultans! At the centre of the bridge, which spans the river only a few metres above the water, is a marble plaque inscribed in the flowing characters of the Arabic text. The entire bridge is extremely graceful with its background of green hills and water-meadows, and it seems quite incongruous to see it carrying so much twentieth-century traffic. Mehmet-Pasha's eyebrows would surely have been raised to see it so heavily used, though he might well have enjoyed reading the account of Turkish life under his domination in the Nobel Prize-winning book *Bridge on the Drina* by his fellow Bosnian Slav, Ivo Andrić.

On the way to Zagreb through Bosnia lies Bihać. This ancient town, mentioned as early as 1260, became during the Turkish occupation the most westerly 'outpost-of-empire'. Often attacked by Austrians and Hungarians, it held on firmly, defended by an extra-strong garrison of Turkish troops until

1878 at the very end of declining Turkish rule. It is an attractive old place with a nice legend. It says that there were three sisters, Bika, Seka and Krupana. Each of them built a castle and Bika, whose name means a female bull, but not a cow(!), built her castle at Bihać, the strongest of the lot. It is an attractive small town and there are the remains of a second castle, called Sokolac, which according to the legend was built by sister Seka.

Bihać, on the River Una, has always been an important gateway into Bosnia from the south and west, and was mentioned in a charter granted by King Bela IV — he who ended up in Trogir pursued by the hordes of Genghis Khan. Later, Bihać came into the possession of Hrvoje Vukčić-Hrvatinić whose seat was at Jajce. Then the Frankopan princes of the island of Krk gained control, so close were its early links with Dalmatia and Croatia as well as Bosnia. Its gothic fifteenth-century church of St Anthony was later turned by the Turks into a mosque and, until 1863, the old church tower served the Imam as a minaret.

The River Una on which Bihać is built is wide and there are shallow falls with a large watermill still working there. All the local farmers are allowed to use the mills to grind their corn; there is one mill reserved for maize and another for wheat flour. It is fascinating to watch this age-old process unchanged even in the twentieth century, and to see the fish in the river. The local authorities have recently built a restaurant and motel almost spanning the river. It is called 'Sunce' — sunshine.

So, through the centuries, Bosnia was pulled this way and that, twisting and turning for its very survival. But it still has the atmosphere of a very old country that has seen good things and bad, and has come through with the age-old traditions of kindliness and hospitality intact.

CROATIA

Inland, Croatia is a mixture of farmland, big industrial cities, the huge basin of the Sava River, and an upland and mountainous area which forms a formidable barrier as it nears the Adriatic Sea. Zagreb itself, the capital city, is a delightful old town (see Chapter 5) and, just north of Zagreb, there are some places of particular interest in rural, gently hilly surroundings. There are few drawn-out suburbs in Yugoslavia: one is nearly always either in a town or immediately in countryside which makes driving that much more pleasant.

First on any Yugoslav's sightseeing list is Kumrovec near the

Many Zagorje dwellings are still attractively rustic

border between Croatia and Slovenia, the little village where Josip Broz Tito was born. This small hamlet of one main street, with the Broz family home — beautifully kept — towards one end is a quiet and peaceful place. Tito's childhood home, made into a museum in 1952, could be a typical old Sussex or Suffolk cottage with a bread oven, a spinning wheel and a wooden cradle in one room, and a bracket clock on the wall. Upstairs the rooms are small and must have been cramped when all the family were home. But Tito's parents were not, by any means, the poorest in the village. His father owned a horse and cart, and his mother came from Slovenian farming stock. They were thrifty, and the neat cottage reflects their background.

The interior of Croatia is far less known to foreign tourists than the coast, but history has left a litter of castles, and there are a number of spas, many of them developed during the Austro/Hungarian overlordship.

One such spa, only 22 km from Kumrovec, is Krapinske Toplice near the town of Krapina. This area of north-west Croatia is known as Zagorje — 'for the hills' — and the spa, with good hotels, lies in beautiful hilly countryside covered with woods and vineyards. There are many small farmsteads, and a speciality of the area is breeding turkeys on a farmyard basis. Roadside restaurants will always offer this bird together with a kind of cheese-and-pastry dish or *štruklji* (made from the same pastry as *strudel*).

The thermal springs of Krapina produce radioactive water ranging in temperature from 38° to 42° Centigrade. They were used therapeutically by the Romans when the springs were known as Aquae Vivae.

It was in a cave in the hills near Krapina at the end of the last century that the remains of Paleolithic Krapina Man was first discovered. Homo Crapiensis (30,000 to 40,000 years back) is the oldest representative of the human race found in this part of Europe. Not only did they find the man, but there were also ample indications that he trapped animals by digging pits and disguising them so that the quarry fell in. A small museum near the caves shows how Krapinski Man lived, using implements of stone and bone.

To the north of Krapina is the huge Trakošćan Castle. Now a museum, it is one of the most formidable great buildings left from medieval times. Then, on the road back to Zagreb, there is the spa of Stubičke Toplice (*toplica* meaning warm) in the heart of the Zagorje uplands. Lying on the slopes of the Medvednica Mountain, its springs which emerge at 65° are rich in strontium, titanium and aluminium as well as calcium, magnesium and ferro-oxide; and all forms of rheumatic diseases are treated there.

Close by, in Gornja Stubica, is the baroque eighteenth-century country home of the Oršić family, a dynasty that wielded great power in Croatian history. Still intact, this huge house with its furniture is now a museum. So is its wine cellar. Down at the bottom of the cellar steps the traditional salt and

Carts drawn by oxen are often used in the country around Zagreb

Trakošćan Castle not far from Zagreb, now a museum

bread is offered to each visitor. The barrels in the vaults were always filled entirely with estate wine, except for the one on the far right. Only at a second glance does one notice that this barrel has a door in its front face. For this was the 'petting' barrel for the young — a kind of barrel bundling!

Pictures on the walls of the house illustrate the epic struggle of the Peasants' Revolt in 1573 against the oppressive Hungarian overlords of that time. Close by, along a pleasant field path, is the tremendously powerful statue of Matija Gubec who led the revolt and was later martyred. His statue stands against a backcloth of bronze depicting in bas-relief some of the scenes of that revolt. Matija Gubec is still a hero in Croatia.

Close to Stubica, another village visited by thousands of Roman Catholic Yugoslavs each year is Marija Bistrica, a village with a shrine. Not far from Zagreb, the village lies on a steep hill round a green. This is thronged with pilgrims, and stallholders selling holy mementoes on Sundays and on Marija Bistrica's feast day. The huge church, prominent at the top of the hill, is constantly attended by one or more priests. Services are relayed by loud speaker for those who cannot find room in the church and, in summer, open-air masses are held in the field where the mysterious light was once seen.

Marija Bistrica is the best-known and most visited of all the holy shrines in Croatia. Its story goes back to the early part of the sixteenth century. The statue of the Virgin in the church wears the dress of a noblewoman of the Zagorje area, and it was first placed in the chapel of the Holy Rosary about 3 km from the present shrine. But in 1545, during one of the regular Ottoman incursions of the area, the parish priest moved the statue of Mother and Child for safety to the church of Sts Peter and Paul (where the present church now stands). He told no one where it was so that, on his death, it became lost to the world.

More than 40 years later, a priest at Bistrica saw light through the church window after Vespers. He went back into the church and saw the light shining over the choir. It disappeared but, the next day, the statue was where the light had been. Since that time, they say, many prayers have been answered. The archives at Marija Bistrica record 1,109 miracles and graces between 1688 and 1786, and answers to prayers are still being recorded. In the eighteenth century the church was enlarged and re-consecrated to the Virgin of the Snows — Our Lady of Bistrica — and in 1923 the Pope accorded it the title of Basilica Minor.

In the last six years the Virgin Mary has also been reported to appear frequently to some children in a tiny Hercegovinan village called Medjugorje, not far from Mostar. Although the Catholic Church has yet to pronounce on these (almost daily) visitations described by the children, the village has already become a place of private pilgrimage for more than four million believers — many from Ireland — since 24 June 1981. And though Yugoslavia is officially non-religious, there are many excursions organised, both within and from outside the country, to see this small village of Medjugorje which has now become one of the major European Marian shrines.

A different phenomenon is that of the 16 lakes of Plitvice which lie, surrounded by primeval forest, about half-way between Zagreb and the coast. This has been a favourite spot for centuries; in fact, they say that Julius Caesar was Plitvice's first tourist. He had considerable trouble fending off the local tribes!

A day is hardly enough for these remarkable lakes which are each joined to the next by waterfalls and cascades. The interesting thing is that the water has never worn down the lip of a higher lake so that it is lost to the lake below. Due to certain algae the edges continually build up to hold the water in place. The entire area is protected as a national park and the variety of flora and fauna is quite remarkable. There are three hotels built by the biggest lake. No motor-boats are allowed, but there is a small electric train these days to carry those who can't walk well round the biggest lake. But it is the marvellous peace of the place that is so remarkable; the freedom with which birds, insects and tiny water reptiles move about undisturbed. In the forests above Plitvice they say there are parts where humans have never yet been and, on rare occasions, a bear or two has been known to shamble towards the little village near by. This village has an attractive, very rural café-restaurant where you can see all the old wooden farming tools hung on the walls, and where they bake pan bread on a huge wood fire before your very eyes. They also make good Šljivovica there!

Though not as large as Serbia, Croatia's influence on western Yugoslavia has been prodigious, stretching across Bosnia at times, as well as Dalmatia and Istria. Yet it is a gentle country, its people, perhaps, less excitable and volatile than in some parts of Yugoslavia. And it matches very well the quiet, almost introverted, Slovenians — its neighbours through so much past adversity and shared inequality.

SLOVENIA

Slovenia is a small country with less than two million living within its boundaries. You can motor along its length in four hours, and cross its breadth in three. But the Slovenians are an entirely separate and individual people with their own language and literature, their own flag as other Yugoslav nations within the Federation, an airline, a merchant fleet, and a large share of the European Alps. It is only as one climbs the foothills towards the alps in the north-west that it strikes one as a very different country from Croatia, with different architecture and a different outlook on life.

Slovenia borders both Croatia and Hungary in the east where there are plains and big tracts of farming land, and some very ancient settlements. Such a town is Maribor on the

National costume varies with the region; Slovenia has some of the most beautiful

River Drava which runs parallel with its sister river the Sava, towards the Dunav.

Maribor, though not the capital of Slovenia (which is Ljubljana, see Chapter 5) has long been an important centre. There is a prehistoric burial ground, the remains of an Illyrian castle and a Roman *castrum* near by, but the centre of this delightful old town is pure medieval with old houses and quaint streets, its very heart a crowded square with cafés and restaurants. In the middle of the square, and jostled by traffic, is a statue of St Florian — saviour against fire — pouring water from a jug(!) to save the city. In the main street at its widest point there is a whole group of sculptured figures commemorating the successful fight against the Black Death in the Middle Ages.

There are hotels in the town, and others on the nearby mountain (a short bus ride away from the centre). The mountain is Pohorje on which one leg of the World Cup Women's Slalom is held. At the foot of Pohorje, near the bus station, is the country-style Hotel Habakuk. A cable-car will take you further up for mountain air and alpine flowers. There is also a road leading even higher, with a second chalet hotel at the summit and the little church of St Areh, originally eleventh-century. This small church sits in a field of wild flowers and still houses the tomb of Count Henry II who was canonised only one year after his death.

Maribor, though extremely ancient, is also very practical. If you see white fish stencilled in paint on the pavement, follow the signs to the best fish restaurant in town. If you are interested in wines, there are organised excursions from Maribor to wine cellars and vineyards which include a teetotal driver!

The surrounding countryside is littered with famous wines as well as castles. This is the home of the Ljutomer Riesling — known throughout the UK, and there are many other less known but delicious reds and whites, including a specially revered wine called *Arhivsko*, a memorable wine. On these wine tours a stop is made at the hamlet on Janzev Hill where a 200-year-old wine press is still in working order and where, after much 'tasting' a lunch of ham bones and home-made bread is provided to set off the sparkling wine. Another stop is at Jeruzalem where, in my opinion, some of the finest white wine is grown. The story goes that some pilgrims on their way to the Holy Land rested here. They found it so overwhelmingly beautiful and satisfying that they decided to settle on the spot and call this their Jerusalem, going not a step further.

Another village, Slovenska Bistrica, is notable for the fact that the Romans quarried marble here, as well as for the twelfth-thirteenth-century castle. Then, in a wide valley close by, is the baroque eighteenth-century Schloss Statenberg — a huge pile with beautifully designed gardens and fantastic furnishings which include the bed on which the Empress Maria Theresa once slept. The schloss is being renovated as an hotel and is open for visits.

But the place that has, perhaps, more impact than anywhere else in this part of Slovenia is Ptuj, just 29 km south-east of Maribor. The original part of this walled and most ancient city is set on a pinnacle overlooking the medieval town that later clustered round the River Drava below. The earliest settlement of Ptuj actually existed at the time of Philip of Macedon, Alexander the Great's father, more than 300 years BC. To walk up the steep approach road and go through the old gateway is to enter into a different world: a world of old garrisons and dramatic panoramas; of alarums and lookouts. These days there is nothing more alarming than a café-restaurant and a museum there, but these cannot destroy the impact of a place that has seen such ancient civilisation.

There is plenty more in the medieval part of Ptuj down by the river including a Roman statue to Orpheus standing incongruously beside a gothic deanery; and two Mithraic temples, just for good measure.

South-west of Maribor, on the road to Ljubljana, is Celje, today an industrial city but well known to Rome's imperialists who had to defend their boundaries against the Goths. And, before the Roman era, it was the Celts who gave Celje the name of 'Celeia'. It is interesting that, in some of the more remote villages in the Slovenian mountains today, there are still some Celtic words used in the dialect of their Slovenian language. There are records of Slovenians living in Celje from the eighth century, but it was in the fifteenth century that the surrounding walls were built against the threat of a Turkish invasion. In the Middle Ages the town was governed by the Grofs of Celje, but the family became extinct and left the way clear for the Hapsburgs who took over the lands as they did so much of Slovenia.

Today one of Celje's better-known industries is the setting of precious stones in white gold. It is also well known for the excellent freshwater fishing to be had there.

Novo Mesto is another industrial town, about half-way between Zagreb and Ljubljana. Here, among other things, the Renault cars made under licence in Yugoslavia are assembled. Near Novo Mesto, on a charming stretch of the Krka River, is Otočec, a castle surrounded by water and trout, turned into an hotel. This Krka river has nothing to do with that other Krka in Dalmatia. There is also a motel at Otočec for those in a hurry, but the peace surrounding the old castle and its grounds is worth a lot of time.

On the further, western, side of Ljubljana is yet another photogenic pinnacle, Skofja Loka. This ancient enclosed city, over a thousand years old and first recorded in 973, has cobbled streets as steep as Clovelly and just as narrow.

Almost due south of Skofja Loka is Postojna with its huge cave system set in the heart of the mountain. This has become such a popular tourist attraction that the one original small hotel has been rebuilt as an impressive tourist centre near the caves; there are restaurants and amusement places besides.

The caves, however, cannot change and are just as

awe-inspiring as when they were first discovered. And, though there are many exciting caves in different parts of Yugoslavia open to visitors, Postojna is undoubtedly the most impressive both in grandeur and in size. The existence of the caves was already known in the thirteenth century but they were not completely explored until the nineteenth century. These are not just simple caves, but great 'halls' inside the mountain, the 'chandeliers' and 'organs' formed of stalactites and stalag-mites. Altogether the passages and chambers continue one to another for 21 km at different levels, and to help the visitor along, a small open train runs part of the way into the centre. At the very heart of this great system and deep down in the mountain, there is a small pool of water in which small prehistoric 'human-fish' (*Proteus anguinus*), looking a little like ivory-coloured newts and half transparent, still live in utter darkness moving under the shallow water with rudimentary hands and feet.

Travelling on towards Slovenia's narrow strip of coastline near the Italian border, the roads cross rolling farm and parkland and clumps of tall trees to arrive at Lipica. This old country estate has been known for 400 years as the stud farm at which the famous Lippizaner high-school horses, used at the indoor riding school in Vienna, have always been bred. And, though these days there are other stud farms producing these incomparable animals, from stock dispersed during two world wars, it was at Lipica in this small corner of Yugoslavia, that the strain was first produced. After more than four centuries Lipica still continues to breed pure Lippizaners from stallions of unbroken pedigree.

The stud was first formed in 1580 and exclusively provided horses for the famous Spanish indoor riding school in Vienna. It was the pet project of the Austrian Archduke Charles, son of King Ferdinand, who, when governing the littoral province, bought the estate from the Bishop of Trieste. Charles crossed the sturdy local mountain horses with Andalusian stallions and mares; his aim to breed an elegant and intelligent horse with great stamina that could stand up to the strains of high school training as well as draw carriages. How well his idea worked! Over the course of several centuries a particular race of mostly pale grey — almost white — horses has evolved which cannot be mistaken for any other breed. They are quiet, disciplined, teachable and strong.

After the last war only eleven horses returned to Lipica of the old stock, but by careful breeding there are now more than 200 Lippizaners at the stud farm, and recently twins were foaled live for the first time. Apart from the horses kept exclusively for dressage — these are the finest stallions — there are now 50 geldings for hotel guests to ride. The foals are born a dark brown or black, and a few keep this colour throughout their lives, but the majority gain the pearly colouring of their parents as they develop. They run wild with the mares until they are three years old before being kept in for schooling. The fillies are trained to carriage work and the stallions take on dressage.

Going to Lipica really is an unusual experience, whether you stay in the hotel and ride each day, or whether you take an excursion from one of the coastal resorts.

Before reaching the coast of Slovenia at Koper, there is a twelfth-thirteenth-century church on a hill above the small village of Hrastovlje. Inside are murals dating from 1490, some of which illustrate the Dance of Death. These were painted by Johannes de Castua. The church was fortified in the sixteenth

The famous Lipica dressage horses have been bred in Slovenia for 400 years

century. It is interesting too, that a little further south, in the centre of the Istrian Peninsula and beyond the Slovenian border, there is another Dance of Death about 1km from the village of Beram, near Pazin. Here there is an extensive cycle of murals in the cemetery church of Sv Marija dating from 1474 and executed by another master, Vincent of Castua.

There is much to discover in the interior of Yugoslavia. Every journey will bring something new to the discerning traveller.

C·H·A·P·T·E·R·4
Mountains and Lakes for all Seasons

Unlike many countries Yugoslavia has not just one mountainous area but several completely separated from each other, and each composed of a different type of mountainous terrain. As is the geological nature of mountains, nearly all these areas have great rivers and lakes as companions and these high and dramatic places occur in Slovenia, Bosnia, Montenegro, Serbia and Macedonia.

MONTENEGRO: MOUNT DURMITOR AND ŽABLJAK

For Yugoslavs the most evocative range is that of Durmitor in Montenegro. Scenically, the entire spread of the Durmitor mountains is superb. Through it runs the River Tara, one of the least polluted stretches of water in Europe. Over many thousands of years, the Tara has worn the face of the earth away to such a degree that Durmitor now has the second deepest canyon in the world, the Grand Canyon in the USA beating it by only a few metres. The best place to view this natural phenomenon is near the small village of Žabljak — not the Žabljak on an island by Lake Skadar, but the age-old hamlet perched on a huge plateau in the mountains.

Žabljak itself is covered in snow until April but, although there is a little skiing in the area, it is not organised for winter

The Tara Canyon, second only in depth to the Grand Canyon in the USA

sports. It is the summer that sees it blossom, both with hotel guests (there are four hotels) and, almost unbelievably richly, in the fields, which are starred like some firmament with rare and brilliant flowers. At least one species is found nowhere else in the world — a botanist's paradise. And over it all presides the majestic black-and-white figure of Mount Durmitor itself.

There are altogether 18 glacial lakes surrounded by tall forests in this vast upland world. The lakes are teeming with fish which, like the flowers and trees of this huge National Park, are protected. There are marked paths through the forest leading from one lake to another; a few rustic huts and a water-mill or two are kept in repair; and it is the peace as well as the beauty that is overwhelming.

The edge of the Tara Canyon can be reached by road from the village and this, too, is a fascinating journey which passes through upland pastures where young shepherds — as often as not playing a wooden pipe to their sheep and goats — spend their days much as their forefathers must have done since biblical times.

Looking down over the canyon is breathtaking. It is so deep that the eyes will hardly focus on the slim ice-blue ribbon of water winding its way so far below. The trees on the steep sides are varied, some of them growing out of sheer rock. And it is interesting that deciduous trees grow higher up than the firs.

Altogether there are about 87,000 acres to the Durmitor National Park, and the whole has been included in the Unesco list of cultural and natural treasures of the world's heritage. In the further reaches, away from mankind, black bear, wolves, chamois, fox, hare, duck and eagles live undisturbed. Near the top of the canyon there is an ice-cave which, like the edge of the canyon, can be reached on foot.

Durmitor and the village of Žabljak are not places for the 'plush'-minded; the people here are simple, honest and brave. Their numbers were literally halved during the war when the Germans took reprisals on Partisan families. Above the village there is a most poignant small memorial, rather like a squat little stone house, where all the names of those killed are inscribed on the walls — 3,400 of them out of a population of about 6,500.

I climbed up through a field full of wild flowers to this small unpretentious memorial, quietly to look and to ponder. An old Partisan came up to me appearing rather stern-faced. From past experience I realised at once what his thoughts were. I have fair hair — in fact aryan colouring — and I hastened, not only to speak in his language, but to explain quickly that I was English. His face cleared, 'Ah, ti si Engleskinja', and his natural good manners became evident. 'We were always together', he said. 'We must still go on together'. I was British, and therefore an ally who had helped win his country's freedom. I would be ever welcome in his house, and free to anything that was his. The cruelties of the old enemy are still not forgotten in Žabljak.

It was near Durmitor that Col. Sir William Deakin — then Captain Deakin — landed by parachute on 27 May 1943, having flown in from North Africa to head the first British Mission to Tito and his forces. The operation was named 'Typical'. With him came four NCOs and Captain William Stuart. Their first encounter with Tito was actually in the trees just by Crno Jezero — the Black Lake — nearest to the village of Žabljak which German forces were, even then, approaching.

Within a week or two, not far away at Sutjeska, one stick of bombs was to kill Captain Bill Stuart, wound Tito, and cost Colonel Deakin one of his boots, wounding him in the leg.

It was three months after this event that Brigadier Fitzroy Maclean (later Sir Fitzroy Maclean, Bart) parachuted into Bosnia on Churchill's orders to continue the work of the British Mission to Tito. Sir William Deakin's book *The*

Embattled Mountain tells most graphically of those times.

Today the Crno Jezero is a lovely quiet stretch of water. By a path through the trees there is a small plaque commemorating Tito's first meeting with the British. Near the lake the oldest hotel (now renovated and refurbished), was a Partisan hospital during that appalling period of Yugoslav history.

For lovers of unspoilt nature, and for those who value peace, there is no place comparable to Mount Durmitor.

MACEDONIA: LAKE OHRID

In the very heart of the Balkans, far to the east and tucked in behind Albania, Greece and Bulgaria, with Serbia to the north, lie some of the most lovely and secluded lakes. They are surrounded by mountains — some of which are Albanian — but not overpoweringly pressed in by them. A French survey team intimated that the skiing near Lake Prespa, when developed, would be among the finest in Europe, but this has not yet come about. The area is far enough south for the lakes to be accessible and attractive at all times of the year. They are richly stocked with fish, and the air is clear and invigorating. Being so close to both Greece and Bulgaria, the flavour of food is strongly influenced by the long occupation of the Turkish Empire, while Byzantine and oriental building has left its mark throughout the country.

Lake Ohrid was known as Lichnidos to the ancient Greeks. It is 695 m above sea level, and covers an area of about 350 sq km. About 36 km long and 15 km wide, it has a maximum depth of 286 m. This is, in fact, the greatest depth ever measured in a European lake and probably accounts partly for some of its unique properties. On a clear, calm, sunny day the water is translucent to a depth of about 22 m, so free is it from pollution. Fed by springs, some of its water arrives from its sister lake, Prespa, which lies at a higher altitude, while several rivers also run into the lake. Water flows out of Lake Ohrid via the Black Drim River which later joins the White Drim to flow, via Albania, to the Adriatic Sea at Leš on the Albanian coast.

Lake Ohrid teems with fish: there are 17 different species; the best known being two of the many sorts of trout, which are found only in this lake. These fish are excellent to eat, one of them having salmon-pink flesh. Other species include carp, eel, chub, barbel, and a tiny little fish called *plašica*. It is from the scales of this little fish that the attractive 'Ohrid pearls' – looking like mother-of-pearl — are obtained. Ohrid 'pearls' make very attractive and delicate-looking necklaces and other pieces of jewellery, and can be bought from jewellers in the area.

Examination of the flora and fauna of Lake Ohrid has produced some important and fascinating results. It was carried out by a Yugoslav biologist, Dr Siniša Stankovič, over a number of years, beginning in the 1920s. He found that several endemic and completely unkown fish still live in the lake which acts as a reserve of fish and plants long extinct in other areas of the world. Previously, these fish had only been known through their fossils. It is estimated by some biologists that the lake is some 4,000,000 years old, and was formed at about the same period as two other well-known lakes and sources of biological information — Lake Tanganyika in Africa and Lake Baikal in Siberia.

There are three main towns on the shores of Lake Ohrid; they are Ohrid (see Chapter 5) and Struga on the Yugoslav side, and Pogradec on the Albanian shore.

The Illyrians were the first known settlers round this lovely stretch of water; they were there from the twelfth to the fourth centuries BC. These people became acquainted with the ancient Greeks and Greek art as early as the sixth century BC and there have been many finds of gold masks and golden sandals, among other objects, in the tombs of Illyrian princes excavated in the vicinity of Trebenište, a village nearby. In the fourth century, Philip of Macedon seized the shore-side settlements of the lake. Later, during the reign of his son Alexander, Ohrid (or Lichnidos) prospered well under Hellenic culture.

When the Romans arrived in 148 BC they constructed the Via Egnatia linking Dyrrachium, the present-day Albanian coastal town of Durresi, with Salonika and Constantinople through Ohrid and Heraclea Lincestis (near present-day Bitola).

The first Christian missionary to arrive in Ohrid was Erasmus of Antioch who was to prove the forerunner of deep Christian activity in this area of Macedonia until the Ottoman Empire effectively curbed it all. Records state that, as early as the fifth century, there was a bishopric at Lichnidos. Later, the famous Greek Orthodox brothers, Kliment and Naum, disciples of Cyril and Methodius of Salonika, came to the lake — in 886 and 900, respectively — and continued their life's work of creating an ecclesiastic and literary language for the Slav peoples. It is now thought that they based the alphabet on the slightly older Glagolitic script, adapting it into the Cyrillic alphabet later.

Sv Naum's monastery at the further end of the lake from Ohrid town and close to the Albanian frontier can be visited by road or by boat. It is an extraordinarily peaceful place: a peace which the crowds visiting this exquisite gem of Byzantine building never dispel. This monastery, dedicated to the Archangel Michael, was the home and workplace of Sv Naum until 910 when he died. He is buried where he lived and worked. His original church was destroyed during the Turkish period and the present church was constructed on the foundations of the earlier one between the fourteenth and seventeenth centuries. Some of the frescoes in it depict Sv Naum as a lover and tamer of animals.

On the other side of Ohrid town, and 14 km to its west, is Struga, green and pleasant on the shores of the lake. Although the town appears to be very modern, with tourist hotels on the shore, Struga was already a town on the ancient Via Egnatia route to Constantinople. There are the remains of two very early basilicas in the vicinity dating from the fifth century. Both contain fragments of mosaic flooring. A little further on, and almost approaching the Albanian frontier post, are two anchorite chapels, Bogorodica and Anastasia. These chapels were carved out of the solid rock of the steep hillside above the monastery of Kalište, and contain fifteenth-century frescoes.

Lake Ohrid has extraordinary qualities. It seems timeless and, as Ivo Andrić wrote in *Beside the Luminous Lake Ohrid* able to hold the precious fleeting moment indefinitely.

> If you are bathing in Lake Ohrid on a sunny day . . . you will see on the pale expanse all around you silvery, transparent bubbles, big and small. In each of them the sun is doubly reflected, like two focuses of different sizes . . . you can see in it, as in a distorting mirror, the reflection of your face, wet and laughing. And all the time, that bigger sun, like a vast star, hangs over your head.
>
> It all lasts for just an instant, like all beauty, yet it is repeated over and over again.

MACEDONIA: LAKE PRESPA

Lake Prespa is quite close to the bigger lake of Ohrid. Lying 853 m above sea-level, it is 158 m higher, and the trees grow more sparsely near its shores. It is the highest lake in this area of the Balkans and is criss-crossed by the frontiers of Yugoslavia, Greece and Albania. It is an exhilarating place. There are hotels at its edge but, until it comes in to its own as a ski resort, it will probably remain much quieter than Ohrid.

There is an interesting old inscribed stone near the lake, a memorial put there at the beginning of the eleventh century by the Bulgarian king Samuilo. Prespa was his first resting place when, for a short time, he regained control of this Macedonian area which his predecessor, Simeon, had conquered in the nineteenth century, and which had later been lost again to Byzantium and Serbia.

Sadly, this period of conquest and counter-conquest of the Macedonian area carried out by Simeon and Samuilo led to a thousand years of bitterness and bickering between Bulgaria, Macedonia and Serbia. From that period on, Bulgaria felt she had a claim to it, including Ohrid. In both world wars the Bulgarians fought against Serbia, only changing sides at the end of World War II. Yet they are all Slavs with a language which is remarkably similar.

Samuilo was, by and large, a 'good' emperor in the jargon of *1066 and All That*. He had the stone inscribed and put up over the graves of his mother and his brothers which also lie in the vicinity of Lake Prespa. This stone is the oldest ever discovered to have a written text in the Slav language.

On the eastern shore of the lake, in the small village of Kurbinovo, there is the unpretentious little church of St George. Inside this modest building there are some superb frescoes. A note carved near the altar confirms that they are very early — painted in 1191. Belonging to the Comnenian period of Byzantine art, the paintings show slender sinewy figures of great elegance and detail of drapery, and they are considered of such importance by Byzantine art experts that this small unassuming church of Kurbinovo has found itself firmly on the art world's map.

Some much older and grander remains are to be found just off the road between Lake Prespa and Bitola — about 1 km from the latter. This is Heraclea Lincestis, an ancient commercial town on the Via Egnatia. The foundations of many buildings with beautiful mosaic flooring and a number of marble statues have been excavated here in recent years, as well as majestic columns in the remains of this once flourishing centre. It is thought that the earliest settlement, on which Heraclea Lincestis was superimposed, may have been as early as 4500 BC in the Neolithic period. It all lends credence to the possibility that the ancient 'heroes' of Greek legend, as well as the direction of the Amber Route, passed through Eastern Europe this way.

MACEDONIA: LAKE DOJRAN

Lake Dojran is much further east than the other two lakes, and

Heraclea Lincestis, a rich commercial city on the Via Egnatia in ancient times

right in the corner where the frontiers of Yugoslavia, Bulgaria and Greece join. As soon as you set eyes on this strange lake you feel the impact of its timeless atmosphere. It is shallow — only 8 m at its deepest — and the frontier between Yugoslavia and Greece is marked by a line of floating barrels strung across the water.

Until the end of the First World War the nearest port, Salonika (or Thessaloniki) — eastern Europe's important outlet to the Aegean and Adriatic seas — had been fought for variously by different powers for centuries. These powers included Serbia during Stefan and Dušan Nemanja's reign (1331–55), when he was actually crowned 'Emperor and Autocrat of the Serbs and Greeks, Bulgarians and Albanians'. Later, of course, the entire area was all part of the huge Turkish Empire and it was not until the 1914–18 war that it was finally returned to Greece, with the frontier running just south of Dojran. The fighting in this area had been appalling. The Bulgarians fought on the side of the Austrians and Germans against the Allies which included British, French and Serbian regiments. Many of the British had come straight from the Dardanelles (*The Gardeners of Salonika* by the historian Alan W. Palmer describes those days most vividly). The line of battle ran north of Salonika through mountainous country and the old town of Dojran which was burnt down by the Turks.

There is a most impressive cenotaph in memory of those who lost their lives here, together with a French and British cemetery.

In 1920, in place of Stari Dojran, Novi Dojran was built close to the former town. All that remains of the older buildings are the outside walls of the church of St Elijah, and the tower, plus a few walls of some of the old houses. So there is little that is historical to see.

But the real fascination of the place is the lake which provides the people of the area with their only industry, fishing. And what fishing! To say that they fish with birds would be to bring to mind the Japanese way, when a string is tied round the neck of wading birds to prevent them from swallowing the fish they catch with their beaks. The Dojran fishermen do use birds, but they are migratory birds that come down to the water in flocks and chase the fish into a netted corner. The fishermen arrange their nets in strategic places to trap the majority of the fish herded by the birds in their search for food.

The work of the industry starts in October when the 'breaks' and 'corridors' for the birds and fish are constructed with the cane that grows in the lake. They use only natural materials working, as they say, with and not against Nature. Shelters are then constructed with the rushes above the surface of the lake. In November the birds begin to arrive from the north. Most welcome of all the varieties are the cormorants, though several species of duck are also an efficient aid to the industry. The birds chase the fish towards the 'hides' where the fish seek to find shelter among the reeds and are caught in the ready-prepared nets. In December, over a period of 10 to 15 days, around 15 to 20 tonnes of fish are caught in this way. The total catch is strictly controlled and never exceeds 450 tonnes annually, so as not to deplete the lake. Some larger birds are encouraged to come down and feed by the strategic placing of fish where they can be seen in the water. These birds are then netted and have their wing feathers clipped to keep them on the lake all the winter, acting as decoys. In spring, new wing feathers grow, and they fly off to resume their natural life-cycle again.

In summer fishing is done with normal nets and boats, and by hook and line fishing. The largest fish, called a *som*, is rather like a freshwater catfish. Other large fish include carp, and a fish similar to a small red mullet called a *perkina*. Visiting tourists are able to fish the lake by obtaining an inexpensive day permit, but all fishermen are obliged to stay 100 m clear of the frontier barrels on the lake.

All fish professionally caught in Lake Dojran are packed in ice on lorries to be distributed within Macedonia. There used to be many freshwater scampi in the lake as well, but the surface was sprayed one year against mosquitoes. The spray polluted the water, killing the food on which the scampi lived: a sad blow for the local industry. But while birds continue to migrate and catch fish, the people of Dojran can continue to make a living in the old way.

There is a small and very good museum attached to the fishing co-operative's office which shows the fauna and flora of the lake. The fauna includes voles, tortoises, a type of marten or large weasel with webbed feet, water snakes, leeches, etc. Also insects, weeds — and fish!

A Lake Dojran 'hide' where migratory birds assist the fishermen

CENTRAL SERBIA: MOUNT KOPAONIK

The summer and winter resort of Kopaonik in the heart of Serbia is completely new. Modern hotels, ideal for skiing as well as summer stays, and well-furnished apartments of varying capacity, have been built in the last year or two in this previously unknown mountain and valley area. This new 'in' place, Kopaonik, provides comfort, mountain air, good food and superb upland walking in a back-to-nature setting. The surrounding mountains are more like high uplands than alps and are smooth and covered in grass above the tree-line in summer, and blanketed in deep snow in winter. The entire area of Kopaonik, with its small villages in the valleys, has always been a place of shepherds and their flocks, cut off from the outside world. Its people have been comparatively poor, living on the proceeds of milk and cheese production, and home-spun wool. Those living on the further side of the area suffered in the past from earthquakes, too. This was why, at the beginning of the 1980s, the authorities decided to breathe new life into this lovely and isolated area, with the aid of planning and financial help from one of Belgrade's biggest enterprises — General Export, parent company of, among others, Yugotours.

I have yet to see Kopaonik in winter, but in 1986 I was there in summer, and it is easy to see why it will become a popular skiing resort. The mountains are wide and smooth, without trees or big rocks in the top reaches. The snow fields are wide enough for the most timid of beginners to traverse. The arrangement of ski-lifts — thirteen altogether, five of them chair-lifts working in summer as well — will provide interesting runs even for the most expert. Altogether there are 33 km of pistes, the longest single run being 2.5 km. At the same time, because the snow fields are so wide, there is plenty of room for small children and tobogganing.

In summer the carpet of grass covering these uplands is cropped by the sheep to resemble green velvet, and there are clumps of violets and other flowers which, unaccountably, the sheep don't spoil, growing between tall groups of firs and spruces. Among the trees are ancient wooden huts or tiny one-room cottages entirely constructed in rough wood. In summer the owners of these huts occupy them for four months of the year. The buildings are known as *bačije*, and a couple will arrive, complete with flock of sheep, stores, cows, and perhaps a horse, together with their indispensable sheep-dog, to take up residence. They will build a wood fire to cook on, milk cows and sheep for milk and *kajmak* cheese, spin the wool by hand on a spindle, and move their sheep about as necessary.

The people of the *bačje* live in the same manner as their ancestors have done for centuries; they have a strange, almost kingly, dignity.

We came across one such old couple, both in their seventies but still physically very robust, who were delighted to have some fresh company. They pressed us to stay, offering milk and cheese. They had two huts: one for sleeping and eating, the other for storing the wooden barrels of *kajmak* and the milk.

At the end of September, when the weather turned, their son would arrive by tractor to take them down to their house in one of the villages. The name of their village is Djordjević; their family name is Djordjević, too!

Now that summer tourism has come to Kopaonik, there are some organised excursions arranged by local mountain guides together with the tourist office. One of these excursions is a five-hour walking and picnic tour to see some of the *bačje* and get a glimpse of their occupants' life. A barbecue picnic among the shepherds is included.

The hotels at Kopaonik have been built with young skiers in mind, with open log fires and music in the evenings. The new apartment village is attractive for people of all ages, whether skiers or not. Built round a triangular open space, there are restaurants, shops, a supermarket, cafés, and a ski-hire shop which is separate from the hotels. It is an attractive complex with apartments containing from two to six beds, a two burner stove, a refrigerator, and everything from bed-linen and cutlery, plus some service, provided.

Perhaps most important of all for Kopaonik, the airport at Niš has been enlarged and opened to civil aircraft, making the arrival and transfer of visitors from other countries much easier.

Bosnia: The Mountains of Sarajevo

Bosnia's mountains leapt to fame at the time of the 1984 Winter Olympics. In many ways the skiing fields and runs are in an ideal position, being very close to Sarajevo and its Olympic-sized airport. And because there are several mountains of different types, Sarajevo can accommodate all forms of winter sports. Mount Jahorina is the best known and has been established for some years as a down-hill skiing resort. It is about 29 km by road from Sarajevo, and the hotels are in the middle of the ski slopes, with the top station of one chair lift just below. Altogether there are five chair and five drag lifts, and the skiing is mostly suitable for intermediate and fairly inexperienced skiers. But there is the Black Run down from the top station and the Olympic Ladies Down Hill; Slalom and Grand Slalom runs connect with the lifts for the macho-minded.

A second mountain, Igman, is only 25 km from Sarajevo, and here the Olympic cross-country skiing course was laid out. There are 60 km of cross-country, or Nordic, skiing here, and a very good modern hotel. When you want a change, a shuttle bus will take you to a third mountain, Bjelašnica, the highest in the area. Mount Bjelašnica was the venue for the Men's Olympic Down Hill and Slalom events in 1984, and it provides superb runs for the really experienced skier.

Though the mountains round Sarajevo are mostly regarded as a winter sports centre, Mount Igman does have a summer season. The terrain is wooded and fairly flat for walking, but the air is alpine. At the same time Sarajevo, with its minarets and other oriental attractions, in the valley below fairly quivers with heat in summer.

These days, new roads built partly for the Olympics make the coast and even Dubrovnik a journey of only three or four hours.

SLOVENIAN ALPS: LAKE BLED

The best-known lake resort in Slovenia is Lake Bled. Here you have a background of high alps, a lovely sheet of deep water, a castle reflected from the heights, and a small lake island supporting an early Christian foundation. Bled is a model alpine centre; there are wooded walks, boating, bathing and mountaineering at hand. And the small lakeside centre of the town has plenty of cafés, souvenir shops and other amusements. In summer there are fiacres to take you about; in winter there are sleighs and horse races on the lake when it has frozen deep enough.

Bled is a spa, and its springs emerge from the lake just in front of the oldest hotel, the Toplice. In fact the hotel's indoor swimming pool comes ready heated from the thermal spring at 23° C! To cope with its popularity — the Duke of Windsor went there before the last war, among many other well-known figures — many hotels have been built. Some are down by the lake, and others are a little higher among the tall trees. The most recently opened hotel is a super-luxury affair a little further along the lake in the residence which was once the royal family's Slovenian retreat, and later President Tito's alpine home.

With a high season in both summer and winter, Bled is busy all the year round. There is a golf course and horse-riding close by. To ski entails a bus ride from the town's hotels to the other side of the lake.

The castle has a fairy-tale look and is now a museum. There is a restaurant with tables and chairs spread out on the wide terrace high above the lake. It is an interesting place to visit which still has a lot of atmosphere. It was the palace of the bishops of Brixen. The lands around Bled were presented to the bishop in 1004, and there is a copy of the original deed in the castle museum. Some of the furniture is well worth seeing, too. Outside the old walls it is the view of the lake below, with its backcloth of high alps, that really takes the breath away while, from the other side of the lake near the town centre, the perfect reflection of the old castle on a sunny day is one of the most photogenic sights.

Slovenian mountain food is always excellent, and their coffee and cream cakes are memorable. There is trout from the lake and wood strawberries in summer; it is hard not to eat too much. But there is always a stiff upland walk to put things right, or a meander at lake level to the Vintgar waterfalls descending from sheer rock: a walk of 4 km from Bled.

SLOVENIAN ALPS: BOHINJ

There is a second summer and winter, alpine and skiing,

Bled Castle, once the seat of the medieval Bishops of Brixen

centre just 29 km away from Bled at Bohinj. Bohinj Lake is long and narrow, with an onion-spired church at one end for good measure. The village is small, and the hotels are, with one exception, dotted round the shores of the lake. The exception is a skiing hotel by the top station of the cable-car on Mount Vogel, part of the huge Triglav massif. The cable-car works all the year round, so that visitors on lake level can reach the mountain heights in a few minutes in both summer and winter. Mount Triglav is Yugoslavia's highest mountain, beating Mount Durmitor by a few metres. The skiing is well catered for at Bohinj, particularly for intermediate skiers, though the nursery slopes are not very extensive. In summer the walks round the lake and on the heights are full of interest. At the far end is the Savica waterfall plunging vertically into a deep pool — one of the two sources of the Sava River. The second source rises in a shallow pool as a spring on the other side of Mount Triglav near Vršić, and joins its sister source near Lake Bled.

SLOVENIAN ALPS: KRANJSKA GORA

The best-known winter sports resort in Slovenia — though every mountain in the region is skied down by Slovenians — is Kranjska Gora, very close to the Austrian border. This skiing centre sees the World Cup skiers every year on their circuit for Slalom races, and also for the huge ski jump that is so close by. Skiers of all standards and all ages flock to this resort. The nursery slopes are wide, with a children's drag lift as well as the normal ones. There are, altogether, four chair-lifts and 15 drag-lifts in the area, and 'black' or difficult runs as well as a number of intermediate. There are 22 km of marked pistes, and the longest of them descends 800 m in a distance of 3 km.

Kranjska Gora caters for *après-ski* life better than other resorts, with discos, tavernas, dancing, and even a night club in one of the hotels, while one down-hill piste is floodlit at night.

There are three skating rinks, and there is curling. In the village there is a ten-pin bowling alley. Near the hotels on the flat stretch at the foot of the nursery slopes horse-drawn sleighs wait to take you for a ride on the snow; the horses good-temperedly put up with an enormous amount of attention from people both on and off the skis. I imagine the hotels must gauge their weekly consumption of sugar, taking the horses into account!

Apart from alpine skiing, Kranjska Gora has three cross-country courses for ski-trekking, the longest of them 22 km.

Being so close to the Austrian and Italian borders, there are organised day-excursions to both Villach in Austria and Tarvisio in Italy. Both entail a very beautiful coach drive, whether in summer or winter. Another excursion goes on a visit to the Elan ski factory where there is a museum of ancient skis which includes some of those worn by Partisans during the war. These are very different from those turned out by this modern factory today and used so successfully by that world-master of the slalom, Ingemar Stenmark of Sweden, as well as by top-class Yugoslavs.

Kranjska Gora also has plenty of summer visitors, both in its hotels and in private rooms. There is superb alpine air and the broad valley affords plenty of flat walking, as well as mountain rambling. The people are friendly, kindly and helpful. They also make an excellent *Kuhano Vino* (Glühwein) with both red and white wine.

SLOVENIAN ALPS: BOVEC

On the other side of Mount Triglav from Bohinj and Bled, and very close to the Italian frontier between Tarvisio and Cividale, is Bovec, a different resort in many ways. The village lies at the foot of Mount Kanin in the beautiful valley of the River Soča which has such an outstanding variety of flowers and shrubs that it has been designated a protected area.

In winter Mount Kanin has a very good snow record. The skiing is best suited to intermediate and expert skiers, though there is a ski-school on some nursery slopes. It is well provided with lifts, including a four-seater gondola up from the foot of the mountain in the village of Bovec, rising to 2,202 m with two intermediate stations. From here the two longest runs drop 1,326 m. At the very top there is a restaurant with the most spectacular views, and it is from this point that the testing Alpine ski tours start out. There are also plans to combine the pistes on Mount Kanin with those on the other side of the mountain frontier in Italy so that skiers can ski on both sides of the mountain. Apart from alpine skiing there are cross-country tracks in the valley.

Bovec has the most extensive high-altitude skiing in Yugoslavia and is becoming very popular. But, for many visitors, summer is the time to explore the Soča valley and its natural beauties. The climate in the valley is very mild in spring and summer and, further south, even supports Mediterranean shrubs and trees such as oleander, cypress and olives. But near Bovec the flowers are alpine and profuse, and the river valley is lush with vegetation. Not far away, near the hamlet of Trento, there is a statue set on a small hill with, sitting and gazing along the valley, the figure of Dr Julius Kugij (1854–1944). Dr Kugij spent the greater part of his life exploring the Soča Valley and classifying the fauna and flora.

C·H·A·P·T·E·R·5

Famous Cities: Inland and on the Coast

BELGRADE

Belgrade is the Federal capital of Yugoslavia, and the capital city of Serbia. Strategically situated at the junction of the Sava and Dunav rivers which flow to the Black Sea as the Danube, it is not surprising that, throughout history, there have been battles and takeovers.

The city is now in two distinct parts — Old Belgrade on the higher ground and sloping down to the river via its Bohemian quarter, and New Belgrade, built post-war. The latter has been well spaced out with tall concrete and glass buildings, and houses most of the administrative offices of the Federal state, many tall blocks of flats, the huge Sava Centre and conference complex on the banks of the river, and some of the most luxurious of Belgrade's hotels — also built on the landscaped river banks. Another feature on the river is the Ada summer recreation and sports centre, built on an island. There are pools, boats for hire, children's areas and restaurants — even horse-riding. And Belgrade's families flock to it during the hot summer months.

But for visitors, it is nearly always the older parts of the city which attract; and there is plenty to see in old Belgrade which still stands tall, though its walls are pock-marked by the terrible bombing and fighting of the last war.

Kalemegdan is an ancient fortress standing over a bend where the two rivers of Belgrade meet; its tallest landmark the statue of 'The Spirit of Victory'. The fortress is a huge defence system, built up over hundreds of years, with a labyrinth of tunnels and gun-ports, Roman arches and stone chambers, much of it underground through the silt of history. Nearby is a splendid mausoleum occupied by Ali-Pasha — one of Belgrade's better overlords — serving as a reminder of the long struggle of the Serbian people towards freedom after Kosovo Polje in 1389 until the nineteenth century.

Meštrović's 'Spirit of Victory' on Kalemegdan, looking as tall as Nelson's column, has his back to the city. He is naked, and his sword handle protrudes horizontally from his body. In the early 1900s the ladies of Belgrade objected to this suggestive object and insisted on his turning his back to the city!

There are many things to see and organised excursions round the city make sightseeing easy, collecting people from the hotels. There is a zoo, numerous churches of different denominations, and some excellent museums, not least the gallery showing replicas of some of Yugoslavia's finest

Ivan Meštrović's controversial 'Spirit of Victory' presides over the confluence of Belgrade's rivers

frescoes — a worthwhile foretaste for those who intend to study the originals at a later date.

The tours of the city include a drive up the long, tree-lined hill past the foreign embassies and ambassadors' residences, to culminate at 'The House of Flowers' where President Tito rests, in the grounds of his Belgrade residence close to a small garden villa where he loved to work. His tomb, marked by a huge block of plain white marble, lies at the head of an indoor garden, absolutely and always filled with plants in full bloom, and guarded by four soldiers in dress uniform. Close by is his workroom in the little villa, with an old-fashioned microphone still on his desk. Surrounded by trees and birds, it is a place of constant pilgrimage.

A memorial and a mausoleum of a very different kind can be seen a few kilometres south of the city on one of the excursion routes. At the top of Mount Avala, 511 m above sea-level, is a huge and magnificent memorial to the Unknown Warrior. Completed in 1938, it is one of Yugoslav sculptor Ivan Meštrović's most impressive works. For it he carved in granite the figures of four women — many times life sized — in the national dress of each one's area. They stand like caryatids and their faces, unsmiling, show a steadfastness that is overwhelming. On this same excursion from Belgrade, a visit to Topola, at the foot of Mount Oplenac, brings you to the church and mausoleum where members of the Karadjordje dynasty of Serbian kings are buried. The contrast between this grand mosaic and fresco-filled building and President Tito's simple flower-filled resting place is startling.

The route back to Belgrade passes Grocka on the River Dunav. It is an attractive area where many Belgrade families have built their weekend cottages. There is also an excellent restaurant specialising in the best Serbian dishes and wines.

Back in the heart of old Belgrade is Duchess Ljubica's house, big, completely Turkish and now a museum. Here the Duchess Ljubica was installed when she was rescued from a harem by Duke Michael who led an uprising against the Turks in 1831. It is a charming house.

Being a capital city, Belgrade has many night-clubs as well as theatres, ballet and opera. Restaurants are legion, providing for all ethnic tastes with music varying from the gypsy-Hungarian, through oriental-flavoured Serbian folk music, to the noisy Western. But it is to Skadarlija that many people gravitate.

Skadarlija is unique. An old quarter of the city with steep cobbled streets — some closed to traffic — small rustic-looking houses, and even an old brewery. Thanks to the imaginative vision of a Director of Tourism, the entire quarter — a kind of *Quartier Latin* — has been renovated with cafés, some of the best restaurants, and a centre where young artists can sell their work. As well as tourists, students congregate of an evening, strolling down the streets and dropping into a *kafana* to drink and discuss the world with their friends. In winter, a restaurant may sometimes light a brazier outside and offer *Šumadijski Čaj* — Foresters' Tea — made of Šljivovic, sugar and boiling water; a most warming drink! And a 'forester' may fire his shot gun (filled with blanks) into the air to ward off evil spirits. Later, a 'fortune-teller' may appear (in costume, hot from singing at the Opera House) to tell the future. It is all such fun. But then this is the spirit of Belgrade. It is a light-hearted city second to none.

CETINJE

Although Cetinje has been superseded since the last war by Titograd in the plains, it was for generations the eagle's-nest capital of Montenegro and, whereas Titograd is a modern post-war commercial city, Cetinje is so full of past history that it really is a museum town.

These days it is quiet and sleepy, although there is a factory making refrigerators, etc., giving work for the inhabitants. The main street holds no less than 14 erstwhile embassies, thanks mostly to Montenegro's only king, Nikola. He was 19 when he came to the throne in 1860, where he stayed until 1918. Nikola was, in many ways, a remarkable man and he earned the title of 'father-in-law of Europe' by marrying most of his nine daughters into the royal families of European kingdoms, including Italy, Germany, Russia and Serbia. Of course, each son-in-law needed an embassy, which considerably heightened Montenegro's status in the hierarchy. Among these embassies, the French building is notable for its Egyptian style. The story goes that the French authorities in Paris made a mistake, sending the materials intended for Cetinje to Cairo, and vice versa.

At the far end of the little town, and spaced out among trees, a park, and a grassy square there is the royal palace, now a fascinating hotch-potch of furnished rooms, memorabilia, swords, portraits, royal gifts and princesses' bedrooms, plus a valuable library — all on show as a museum with a guided tour. Opposite is the prince bishop Petar Petrović Njegoš's residence. This is also a museum, with some of Njegoš's possessions — his *gusle* (stringed instrument), his chair, etc — and an ethnological collection with costumes, implements, and so on. Quite near is the monastery of which he was *Vladika* or Prince Bishop; it still works as a monastery today. This building was the seat of government as well as religion in Montenegro for almost 400 years.

It is said that Cetinje's beginnings came about in 1450 when some shepherds, banished for political wrong doing by the fifteenth-century Serbian ruler, Stefan Nemanja, eventually arrived in the area. They came with their flocks across the mountains to a karst plain, high up and surrounded by peaks. Here these *Vlachs*, or *Morlachs*, who were left over from a tribe of Roman nomadic shepherds and drovers, built a church in 1450, known even now as the *Vlaška* church, Cetinje's first building. Altered and extended, it is now surrounded by iron railings put there in the nineteenth-century. These railings are the barrels of Turkish muskets taken in battle, and if you examine them closely, you can see the original sights still in place on the hollow rods that form the railings — more than two thousand of them. In the churchyard there are two Bogomil gravestones. In 1482, 32 years after the church was built, the ruler of Montenegro (or Zeta, as it was formerly called) came to this high plain at Cetinje in retreat from the Turks. This ruler was Ivan Crnojević, who had previously established his capital on Lake Skadar. He built his palace at Cetinje in 1482 and, two years later, built the monastery in which he installed the Zeta Metropolitan. As a dynasty the Crnojević rulers were forward-looking and they quickly enlisted the help of Venice in trying to keep Montenegro free from the Ottoman Empire. They also installed the first printing press in the South Slav lands, in 1493. Buying the press from Venice, they placed it at Obod with a monastic foundation. And the 'bed' of this ancient press can still be seen near the old chapel of Obod monastery, just above Rijeka Crnojevića and up a winding country road. The press, working not much later than Caxton's famous press, printed the first books in the Cyrillic alphabet.

Later, after a long hiatus during the Turkish occupation that surrounded Cetinje, Montenegro — with the help of Russia — planned once more an independent and self-sufficient state. Danilo, founder of the Njegoš dynasty, became bishop and ruler of the Cetinje diocese. The famous 'annihilation of the converts to Islam' took place, inspiring Danilo's successor, Petar Petrović Njegoš II, to write the epic dramatic and philosophical poem *Gorski Vijenac* — The Mountain Wreath.

Petar II, prince bishop from 1830 to 1851, has been a hero in Montenegrin eyes ever since. He was a simple man of well over two metres in height — a thinker and philosopher as well

*The Orthodox monastery at Cetinje from which the Vladika ruled for
nearly 400 years*

as bishop and ruler. In 1838 he built his 'residence', calling it
Biljarda because he installed a billiard table in one of its
rooms. Until that time — a period of 354 years — all temporal
as well as religious duties were carried out within the
monastery.

Petar Petrović built the first elementary school in Cetinje
and, in 1848, a theatre which is at the present time being
repaired.

After Njegoš's death, his successor Danilo replaced the title
of *Vladika* with 'prince'. His short rule (1852–60) was fraught
with clashes against the Turks. At one time, so short of
ammunition were the beleaguered garrison of Cetinje, the lead
roof of the 'Biljarda' and the metal type of the Cetinje printing
press were melted down for bullets. But from 1860, under
prince (later king) Nikola's diplomatic guidance, Cetinje
became a stable royal city and cultural centre well known in
Europe.

The real hero in the eyes of most Montenegrins, however,
has always remained their poet Petar Petrović Njegoš. His
tomb at the top of the high mountain above the Bay of Kotor,
where he asked to be buried, is a place of pilgrimage; so is the
village of Njeguši in which he was born. He could not marry,
being an Orthodox Bishop, but the people of Montenegro like
to link his name romantically with another poet, a beautiful
woman: it suits the Montenegrin fierce but sentimental soul so
to do.

LJUBLJANA

It is easy to understand why Ljubljana, the capital of Slovenia, has for so long been an important centre and cross-roads in this part of Europe. It lies only 293 m above sea-level in a basin-like valley between the European alps and the karst mountains which form a natural barrier in front of the Adriatic Sea. Roads and railways, not to mention descending aircraft, travel through the 'Ljubljanska Vrata' — the Ljubljana Gate or Gap — which is only 1 km wide and hemmed in by alpine foothills on either side, its floor washed by the Ljubljanica River which flows into the Sava.

Early Neolithic man found the Ljubljana Gap convenient to live in. So did the Illyrians, who left a superb vase of about 500 BC among other things, now in the National Museum. The Romans fortified the area in the time of Augustus and formed a garrison in the town which they called Aemona. A Slav community settled there in the seventh century and, by 1220, there was a sizeable city which nestled by the river at the foot of the hill on which the castle still stands.

The seventeenth and eighteenth centuries saw some of Ljubljana's finest buildings erected, and it is they which give the oldest part of the town its established, solid and prosperous flavour. There are many baroque churches, rich merchants' houses and mansions in this nucleus of the city. When Napoleon, for a short period, formed his 'Illyrian Provinces', Ljubljana became its capital city, but it was Austria, in the days of the Austro-Hungarian Empire, that superimposed its oppressive influence on Slovenia.

Thirty-five years after Napoleon's final defeat, Ljubljana was reached by what was, at that time in 1849, known as the 'Southern Railway', bringing to it a new era of modern accessibility. Since the last war, Ljubljana's suburbs have spread very quickly so that now about one-sixth of the total population of Slovenia lives within the town's limits.

These days, the approach from east, west or south is undistinguished, owing to the influx of homes, schools and factories. This gives little idea of the charms of the old centre with its attractive river running through it, and its old squares and narrow streets.

This part of Ljubljana is dominated by the castle, now open as a tourist attraction. Below, near the river, is the splendid town hall first built in 1484 and altered at the beginning of the eighteenth century, its arcaded court lavishly decorated. There are churches, lovely bridges, an 'Illyrian Column' — memorial to Napoleon's Provinces — the Gruber and other palaces, university buildings and many beautiful art treasures, as well as theatre and opera.

Some of the best restaurants are along the towpath near the River Ljubljanica with its 'Shoemaker' and other bridges. These restaurants serve mainly Slovenian specialities, including smoked hams from venison, and a salami from bear meat and from wild boar. Slovenia's *tortas* are famous and full of fresh cream.

The shops in the old city are many, some of them boutiques for leather goods which are reasonably priced and produced locally. One of the more unusual markets is that where medicinal herbs are sold.

Among Ljubljana's festivals are a mass marriage ceremony in summer with brides and grooms in national costume. On occasion, some Scottish pairs have also arrived in highland dress to plight their troth on this happy occasion. Other events in national costume take place on the river.

Ljubljana is such a friendly city, it is worth a stay, rather than the dash through accorded by most people on their way south.

Ohrid

Ohrid, known to the ancient Greeks as Lichnidos, is not just an attractive lakeside town in Macedonia, but a centre of tremendous character and charm which has gathered to itself a conglomerate of Macedonian and oriental houses, churches, mosques, bazaar stalls and Turkish and fishermen's cafés. For the visitor there is endless fun bargaining for souvenirs from the stalls, searching through the silver filigree shops, seeking out Ohrid 'pearls', and trying on the local leather peasant slippers — or *opanci*. The people of Ohrid are gentle and friendly — like all Macedonians — and happy to talk and explain. Some wear oriental dress, while others still put on their colourful and complicated national dress.

Macedonian folk dances and *kolas* (danced in a long line and sometimes a circle) are fascinating, depending a good deal on balance, and much handkerchief twirling by the leader. Their folk songs employ an eastern melodic minor scale, plaintively tonal, and tell of past sadnesses and heroic deeds. In summer there is an international folk festival in Ohrid.

Bathing in the lake in summer is pleasant, and boating is delightful. The hotels are spread out along the shores and there is a wide promenade planted with roses in front of the old Palace Hotel.

From an historical point of view, Ohrid is most famous for its early medieval and Byzantine buildings, and any lovers of Byzantine fresco and iconic art put Ohrid as a 'must' on their list of visits.

At the top of the steep hill overlooking the town are the remains of Samuilo's fortified castle and its surrounding walls, which enclosed the entire town at the end of the tenth century when Ohrid became his capital and the seat of the new patriarchate. The high ramparts and massive towers of the fortress still remain and, until 1912, the gates in the walls were closed at sunset and opened at dawn every day. In 1912 the Turks, who had ruled the area for 500 years, finally retreated and the gates have remained open ever since.

When Kliment, disciple of Cyril and Methodius, came to Ohrid in 886 he introduced religious services in the Slav language. He also founded a monastery, Sv Panteleimon, and built a church. The monastery, though later turned into a mosque by the Turks still remains, but the Sv Panteleimon church was reduced to its foundations, now carefully preserved. Close by are the remains of an even earlier fifth-century basilica with considerable areas of mosaic flooring, and some fragments of frescoed walls.

The biggest and most impressive church is the cathedral of Sofija, probably tenth century, with its priceless eleventh to fourteenth-century frescoes. The building is very large with structural alterations of a later date. It, too, became a mosque, and many of the lovely frescoes were plastered over and whitewashed. Amazingly, this covering — now cleaned off — preserved the frescoes and their colours, some of which, particularly a certain blue, could never be replaced, as the secret of their making has been lost. In the same way, other frescoes have been preserved by the deposits of votive candles whose grease, now removed, has once again revealed these marvellous colours.

In Sveta Sofija the oldest of the frescoes are near the altar where, among the figures, are the founders of the Cyrillic alphabet.

The smallest of these lovely Byzantine churches is Sveti Jovan, a little outside the town, and tiny. For me it is the most endearing of them all. To reach it there is a small path quite high above the lake, with Sveti Jovan standing alone at the end of a point. It has a symmetry that is quite beautiful. Built entirely of terracotta brick, including its domes and arches, it is of cruciform shape. There are no records of how this small church came into being. Inside, it is richly painted with the figure of Christ Pantocrator and eight flying angels gazing

Sveti Jovan above the shores of Lake Ohrid; a perfect example of Byzantine building

down from the cupola. The painting of the Apostles' communion shows angels in imperial dress, a very unusual feature; while, together with Sv Kliment, there is a portrait of Erasmus of Antioch, the third-century missionary who came to Ohrid. This is the only representation of him among Ohrid's frescoes.

There is so much to see and wonder at in Ohrid, including a newly discovered classical Greek theatre near the fortress. Yet it is a town of today — happy, smiling and flourishing.

SARAJEVO

Until 1984, when the Winter Olympic Games were held on the mountains just above Sarajevo, the most that many people outside Yugoslavia knew about Sarajevo was that it triggered the First World War when the Austrian Archduke Ferdinand and his wife were assassinated on a bridge in the middle of the city. Now, the footprints of that poor little assassin, Gavrilo Princip who was a student still in his teens, are enshrined in cement on the pavement by the bridge; for he was always a hero to the downtrodden and hard-oppressed people of Bosnia and Hercegovina, of which Sarajevo is the capital city.

Travelling through Europe, either north and south, or east and west, the route through Yugoslavia crosses Sarajevo. It is one of the oldest centres of population in the Balkans, peopled for more than 4,000 years. In AD 9 the Romans routed the Illyrian people of the area and set up an administrative centre at nearby Ilidža, where thermal springs are still in medicinal use today with hotels spread out in the park around.

The area continued to expand from Roman times until, in the reign of Stjepan Tvrtko in the fourteenth century, it reached its medieval zenith. But it didn't stop there. In 1435 the Turks finally overran the region. The first Turkish ruler, Isa-Bey Ishaković, built a bridge across the River Miljačka, joining two small villages, and on the left bank built his seraglio, barracks for the troops, government buildings, and the first mosque — the Emperor Mosque. A hippodrome and public baths were added. One the right bank of the river he built a caravanserai, shops and workshops. He also installed the first water and sewage system. The result was that Sarajevo rapidly became one of the most important trading centres in the Balkans, with many highly intelligent and perspicacious merchants and entrepreneurs.

Sarajevo's growth continued under Skender-Pasha and his son. In the sixteenth century Gazi-Husrev-Bey — his uncle a Hercegovin prince and his mother the daughter of Sultan Bayazid — put the finishing touches to both buildings and prosperity in Sarajevo. He built the Husrev-Bey mosque and madrassa, an elementary and a secondary school, a school of philosophy, a library, a free kitchen, and inns.

It is all these fascinating oriental buildings, and the markets in the old quarter, that draw so many sightseeing crowds to Sarajevo. The old quarter of Baščaršija — not far from the Gavrilo Princip bridge — is a complete small oriental village which, though it has been skilfully renovated, seems exactly as it must have been since the sixteenth century. There are craftsmen, tiny shops with overhanging roofs, a han, the caravanserai — now with several restaurants — and small family dwellings. The drainage system has been completely renewed and in the process the original drainpipes were discovered, still working and made from hollow tree trunks. The renovation, carried out meticulously in the old style, seems only to have enhanced the atmosphere of Baščaršija's past; it is still full of leather, silver and copper ware, carpets and rugs, Turkish coffee and Oriental food.

SKOPJE

Skopje is the capital city of Macedonia. Sadly, it lies in the path of an earthquake-bearing fault in the earth's crust, and has suffered greatly in the past. The first earthquake to be

Fascinating bazaars make souvenir hunting a pleasure in Sarajevo and other towns

recorded was in 518 when Comes Marcilinus, an eye-witness, wrote that geysers and a rift 48 km long and 3.6 m wide appeared. After this catastrophe a new city was built near the existing fortress of Kale — it is believed by Justinian who was born in Skopje. The last huge seismic tremor occurred in 1963. Much of the city centre was then destroyed, and further damaged by torrential rain and flooding which occurred at the same time. But there is still much to see in the old city built on the wide reaches of the River Vardar.

Since the earthquake the centre of the town has been redesigned, with a vast open square flanked by the new PTT building. Just one tiny homestead remained after the disaster, and this has been left in place as a reminder of what the centre contained before 1963. Another building remaining just as it was on 27 July of that year is the railway station — now a memorial to that terrible day — its station clock still pointing its hands to the exact minute when devastation struck.

Otherwise, the town on this side of the river is for the most part very modern with many blocks of flats and shops built with anti-earthquake technology, blending in with the few older buildings which were left intact.

The banks of the River Vardar have been landscaped with grassy banks and promenades, and its waters should never again rise in flood as a system to control the flow has been installed. Across its attractive 'Stone Bridge' is the oldest part of Skopje, dominated by the Kale fortress which has stood there since the sixth century. Near the bridge are the Turkish baths of Daut Pasha which have 13 cupolas and were built on the site of a Christian church which he had pulled down. An old legend says that the baths were never officially opened because the pasha's daughter was bitten by a large poisonous snake and the pasha believed that this was a sign of his God's displeasure over the destruction of the church.

Along Marshal Tito street is the church of St Saviour (Sveti Spas). From the outside it doesn't look very much, but inside it is rich with icons, frescoes and gold leaf. Its most striking possession is the iconostasis of deeply carved wood which comes from the well-known Debar school of wood carving in Macedonia. It took two masters five years to complete and shows biblical scenes and figures portrayed from a local point of view — including Salome in Macedonian dress with the head of St John the Baptist. This little church was built at a time when the Turks decreed that Christian churches could not be taller or more beautiful than the Turkish mosques. So the builders of St Saviour's dug below ground level for their church, and a flight of steps leads down to the entrance.

Of the mosques in Skopje, that of Mustapha Pasha, built at the end of the fifteenth century, is outstanding; his tomb lies in the courtyard. Nearby is the Kuršumli Han. This was once called the lead-covered caravanserai until the Turks took its roof to make bullets! Round the han there is a maze of small streets, filled with oriental craftshops for souvenir hunting.

Skopje, perhaps because of its many past disasters, is a most endearing city, small enough to get to know quickly, and surrounded by fertile countryside.

ZAGREB

Since the days of the Amber Route, Zagreb has been on the map as a junction on the main roads of Europe. Trains, planes, long-distance coaches and heavy transport lorries travelling to the Adriatic, the Black Sea, Greece and the Middle East all pass near this city which is the capital of Croatia.

The town lies on the Sava River just where the last foot-hills of the alps flatten out at the western edge of the huge Pannonian Plain. Surprisingly, Zagreb is only a little north of Milan in latitude, and marginally west of Vienna. It is estimated that its game-rich countryside was inhabited some 50,000 years ago and has been continuously occupied by man ever since.

The older part of the town sits perched on a steep hill, but since 1945, the flat area near the Sava has been built over extensively with apartment and office blocks and one of Europe's biggest exhibition centres. Although the Turks never actually crossed the barrier of the Sava to reach Zagreb, the danger of a Turkish conquest encouraged many country landowners, including the powerful Zrinski and Oršić families, to build large town houses within the walls of the old city. It is this area that is of such interest to sightseeing visitors.

The coloured roof of St Mark's church in Zagreb, with its coats of arms, in the old part of the town

164

Here Ivan Meštrović had a home and workshop – now a gallery and museum. Gradec, as it was called, was fortified in the thirteenth century with four town gates; one, the Stone Gate, still survives. The easiest way to go up the steep hill to the old city is by funicular from near the main square, the Trg Republike; it costs little and has been working for about a hundred years.

At the top is the Lotrsčak Bell Tower which used to call citizens in through the gates at night. A cannon still fires every day at noon. Many people live in this attractive part, and the colours on some of the house walls still keep to the original hue. In the old days these denoted the profession of the householder: green for a doctor, yellow for a goldsmith, etc. A wander round, perhaps following the blue and yellow tourist signs, brings you to St Marks. This is not the cathedral, which is lower down and has two spires, but the older thirteenth-century church with the famous coloured roof showing the arms of Zagreb and Croatia. Down Kamenita Street and just in front of the Stone Gate, there is a stone lion and some heavy iron chains. These chains came from one of Nelson's battleships. The covered gateway itself is a religious shrine where a picture of the Virgin was miraculously saved from fire. There are always hundreds of votive candles here.

The descent on foot through the gate takes you by a most engaging country market where, besides flowers and vegetables, they sell cheese and hand-made wooden cooking aids.

A cable car from the town rises up to the heights of Sljeme (1,035 m). Here there are lovely walks through tall trees and several restaurants. It is usually snow-covered in winter.

Within the town are some of Yugoslavia's finest hotels. One of them, the Esplanade, can put on superb banquets in its huge oval hall complete with dark green serpentine pillars, gold plate on the circular tables under its cupola roof, and acoustics as good as St Paul's cathedral. As well as putting on the style in grand hotels, dozens of small restaurants in the town cater for all tastes, whether game, Adriatic or river fish, or Croatian specialities.

There is a beautiful opera house in a green tree-lined boulevard, a number of theatres, museums and art galleries, and a large university. The city was host to an international athletics meeting, in July 1987, of university students from all parts of the world: a kind of students' 'Olympic Games'.

Zagreb is, in every way, a capital city. Its parliament administers the whole of Croatia, Dalmatia and Slavonia; and Croatia and Dalmatia receive about 75 per cent of all Yugoslavia's foreign tourists. Yet, in spite of its importance,

A dance performed near the River Sava

the many small squares and tree-lined roads manage to preserve an air of old-world freshness.

DUBROVNIK

Dubrovnik, known as the pearl of the Adriatic, is unique. An early medieval walled city, it has remained virtually unchanged since it was built. Its massive defence towers, fortresses and encircling walls grew up in the early Middle Ages, but it was first populated as an island refuge by the few surviving inhabitants of Cavtat when they were overrun by Avar tribes in the seventh century. The first defences were of wood, but soon more permanent structures were developed. The people on the island began to trade and prosper, building up a fleet of argosies — those large merchant ships developed specially for overseas trading by the Ragusan (Dubrovnikan) owners. They constructed a causeway across the narrow seawater gap and eventually filled it in entirely. This flat stretch became the city's main street, called Stradun, or the

'Placa'. It is still in use and thousands of tourists today mingle with Dubrovnikans on the marble paving stones which wear the patina of centuries.

Stradun is about 300 m long and very wide with narrow streets and passages running off on either side between the tall medieval buildings that flank its length. By the end of the twelfth century the city had attained its present size. Massive stone walls, wide enough for a hand-cart to travel along, were built, together with fortresses, towers and lazarets which were quarantine quarters for both people and goods arriving by sea. All these vast constructions are still there, and one of the best ways to see the life of the old city, with its churches, monasteries, convents and tall dwellings, is to walk round on the top of the walls, looking down on its busy life.

The whole world comes to see this complete example of a medieval city-state. Sit on the terrace of the Town Cafe and the scene is vibrant with cosmopolitan life. Tourists of all nations, Dubrovnikans with their children, students, market women in national dress all stroll by under the dive-bombing antics of swifts, swallows and pigeons. Gaze at the façades of the cathedral, the Rector's palace, the bell-tower with its green men striking the hours. See Orlando with his sword. His right forearm was used as a standard measure in medieval times; this was a *lakat* or elbow.

Dubrovnik, 'Pearl of the Adriatic' and unique walled city, unchanged by time

Sveti Vlaho holds the model in his hands which helped the
reconstruction of Dubrovnik after the 1667 earthquake

Sitting there you can almost imagine the swish of medieval silken dresses, the clanking of swords, the running of link-boys' feet as you listen to the tinkle of one of Onofrio's fountains. There are two of these, one near the sea-gate and old harbour, and one near the land gate at Pile. The second, near Sv Klara's convent — there is now a restaurant in the cloisters — was used to cleanse the hands and feet of peasants coming in from the countryside. All had to wash in its running water. The fountain is opposite the famous Franciscan monastery which owns the ancient apothecary — still working — dating from 1317 and the third oldest in Europe. The monastery cloisters have stone pillars with delightful carved heads showing their owners' ailments. One poor lady in medieval wimple has toothache!

There are many churches, including an Orthodox church; and one tiny privately-owned synagogue. Outstanding among the churches are the cathedral, built after the earthquake in 1667, and the church of Sveti Vlaho (St Blaise), patron of

Dubrovnik. St Blaise is enshrined in several places in the niches of Dubrovnik's walls. He always holds a model of the city in his hands. It was this representation in silver-gilt, now in the church of St Blaise, which made it possible to rebuild Dubrovnik on exactly the same lines after the earthquake.

Legend says that Richard the Lionheart gave money for the original cathedral to be built in the twelfth century, in thanksgiving for being saved when he was shipwrecked on the island of Lokrum, just outside the old harbour.

The old city has numerous restaurants and cafés; even a night club or two. There are many hotels outside the city walls, all run by one big centralised company. But the city itself, free of wheeled traffic, remains, as it always was — unique.

PULA

It is almost impossible to think of Pula without seeing, in the mind's eye, the huge Roman amphitheatre which stands up on the rise above the wide harbour. It presides over the busy modern city that Pula has become and is a constant reminder of its equally busy past. Open and sunny and situated at the very tip of the Istrian peninsula, Pula has a huge harbour which has been in constant use since Rome's galleys sheltered there and (who knows?) the frail craft of Ulysses.

The amphitheatre measures 132 by 105 m and its outer walls — still largely intact — are 30 m high. It was built mainly to entertain Rome's sailors when the navy was in port, and it had a seating capacity of 23,000. The foundations of three of the many tiers of seats still remain. The towers, built into the outer oval-shaped walls were used for scenic effects for plays and other epics; for example, to simulate rain and even to perfume the arena. Canvas covers, manipulated by 'on duty' sailors, could also be manoeuvred from towers to give shade for the VIPs. The arena floor was of wood, with sand on top to soak up the blood — of lions, of gladiators, or of Christians. The stone supports of this flooring still exist under the arena. Here, too, animals and condemned human beings waited for the performance to begin. There is also a passage at auditorium level along which, it is thought, the gladiators came to the arena from their training college. These days, the arena is used for nothing more bloodthirsty than a film festival.

In the middle of the town there are the remains of the forum, and a temple dedicated to the goddess Roma and the Emperor Augustus. This small building is still in good repair and quite beautiful with its carved friezes and columns. A city gate dedicated to Hercules still stands with his bearded head carved into the arch. And what is so delightful is that there is no roped off area of Pula containing all these Roman remains. People hurry to and fro between them intent on their own business, ignoring the priceless heritage they are used to seeing.

From a later date a Venetian fortress, in very good repair stands on the hill above the town. There are also some notable churches and monasteries scattered about. One of them small, unassuming and Franciscan, houses some really lovely frescoes.

Pula is certainly not just a museum city. There are shipyards, cement factories, a glassworks, knitwear, textiles, furniture production and a thriving tourist industry, with attractive hotels built on the edge of lovely deepwater bays edged with pebble beaches and rock points. Restaurants often specialise in local delicacies — oysters and shellfish like the fat clawless spider-crab. In May, in fact, one of Istria's favourite festivals is the *Fešta od Raki* (dialect) — the Spider-crab Festival.

RIJEKA AND OPATIJA

Large international ports carry a special fascination. All the bustle of passengers, cargo and cars hurrying to get on board, together with the solemn quadrilles performed by the giant cranes, provide endless diversion. But Rijeka has more than that to offer. Behind the wide promenade and the harbour lies the old town. There are many museums, large department stores, an opera house and theatres. The arched gate and clock-tower dating from 1377 serve as an entrance to the older quarter, and from here the town climbs up a steep hill. Half way up this hill is a large, very Italianate building which was used as a seat of government when Italy gained control of Rijeka (Fiume) after the First World War (Treaty of Rapallo, 1920). At this time only the twin town of Sušak was in Yugoslav hands. The European powers who arranged the treaty saw Croatia as just an appendage of the old Austrian empire, rather than as a separate country. The dividing line of that treaty can still be seen at the bridge over the small Rječina river which separated Sušak from Rijeka.

High above the port is the castle of Trsat. An old flight of stone steps built in 1531 gets you there, though a bus is easier on the legs. This castle, which has magnificent views across the Kvarner Bay, was mentioned in the Vinodol Code, and so dates from before 1288. There is a restaurant within the walls, and an open-air stage. The castle was a private home before the first war, when Bernard Shaw was a frequent visitor. His aunt, in fact, was buried in the private mausoleum — built like a Doric temple — and her remains have only recently been reburied in Rijeka.

Near the castle is the parish church of St George, originally thirteenth century, with its walls covered in pictures — some good and some poor — given as offerings by sailor artists saved from the perils of the sea. In a second church, Our Lady of Loretto, lie the tombs of Frankopan princes.

A little to the east, on the coast, is a bay known as Uvala Scot. The land was bought by an Englishman called Scot who left the United Kingdom in political disfavour. His house and stables now form part of an hotel, and the vineyards he planted still produce some of the best sparkling wine in Yugoslavia, *Bakarska Vodica*.

Rijeka has some hotels, but her tourist resort has always been Opatija, about 10 km to the west and favoured, because of its mild climate, by the Hapsburgs when they ruled the area.

Opatija is still *fin de siècle* in atmosphere, though there are sophisticated modern hotels, entertainment, and several night-clubs. Parks filled with sub-tropical plants, elegant façades, a long and attractive promenade, a walk that takes you along the coast just above the sea, and many cafés, boutiques and restaurants, make it a most attractive resort. Above Opatija, on the steep slopes of Mount Učka, there are some very old fortified villages well worth exploring. One is Kastav, 378 m above sea-level; another is Mošćenice, first mentioned in 1374. Both huddle within old walls, with a maze of narrow streets. There are stone-paved squares and ancient communal village wells. Altogether a dip into the past!

On the coast below Mošćenice are two other small resorts: one is Mošćenička Draga; the other is Lovren. The latter won a golden award in 1986 for its Hotel Excelsior. But it is Opatija itself that is the real companion to the port of Rijeka.

ŠIBENIK

Šibenik has a special place in the hearts of many Croatian people — not only because of its medieval centre which is superb, but because it was one of the first Slav towns not to be superimposed on any former habitation. It has a huge natural harbour that is almost landlocked and only the narrowest of sea-channels connects it with the Adriatic. Indeed, so narrow is the channel that vessels can only pass through one at a time, and each must wait for a signal from the port authorities before proceeding.

The old centre of the town rises up steeply from the harbour in layers. Crooked narrow streets, small squares and tall stone houses crowd round its heart which is the superb small cathedral built by that master among stone-masons, Juraj Dalmatinac, and his followers, between 1431 and 1555. This small building is a gem, with its splendid barrel-roof of stone. You can spend a delightful half-hour just going round the outside of the church, gazing at its doorways, and marvelling at the skilled hand that fashioned the small gargoyle faces in their medieval head-dresses. Some of these faces, it is said, closely resemble Juraj's friends; others his debtors and enemies — it is not hard to see which is which!

Inside the cathedral, the master's love of nature is clearly shown in the carving of acanthus leaves which seem almost to be blowing in the breeze. His sense of humour and his understanding of children shine through in his fashioning of the font in the baptistry where two small cherubs are earnestly trying their best in alabaster to hold up the font while the third, a cherubic smile on his face, is making no effort at all!

Outside the cathedral in the square is a beautiful medieval loggia, and the powerful statue of Juraj Dalmatinac himself, sculpted by Ivan Meštrović. From the square, the steep streets and stairways lead up and up past the old houses. Šibenik was often beleaguered, and the crooks and turns in the old streets helped medieval inhabitants to hide and get away to safety.

Settled in the tenth century as a Croatian tribal fortified village, Šibenik was first documented on Christmas Day 1066 when King Peter Krešimir, while in the city, issued a decree guaranteeing freedom and royal protection to a Benedictine convent, Sveta Marija, in Zadar.

Šibenik was twice burnt down by Venice, but only after a prolonged struggle did the Venetians finally conquer it in 1412. Venetian control then lasted for nearly 400 years, and it was during that time that Šibenik acquired so many lovely buildings. There are three castles overlooking the harbour from the high ground above: Sveta Ana, Sveti Ivan and Šubičevac. Sveta Ana is the oldest fortification, and in this oldest part of the town is the Orsini palace, which was owned by Juraj Dalmatinac. At the very top of the hills is the fortified castle of Sv Ivan.

Since the last war Šibenik's modern quarter has expanded a great deal, with aluminium and other factories, and a large commercial section as well as housing estates. The town and its administrators are as independent-minded as ever. When, a year or two ago, the Yugoslav hydro-electric power system was sorely taxed due to drought, the rest of Dalmatia suffered nine-hour power cuts to conserve energy. Not so Šibenik which refused to toe the line. She did conserve energy, but in her own time and way!

SPLIT

Split, half-way down the Dalmatian coast, has been a favourite area of habitation ever since the Illyrian tribe of Dalmatii, who gave their name to Dalmatia, lived there. In a well-favoured and sheltered position — with off-shore islands, a wide outer bay and a completely sheltered inner bay, and with mountains at its back — it is no wonder that the Greeks and Romans found it pleasant, too. They left a wealth of archaeological treasure.

Today Split, with its huge spread of buildings, some referred to as 'The Chinese Wall', beyond the original port and town, is a large commercial, marine and university centre with a population of more than 200,000. A number of hotels have been built on each side of the harbour, some a little way out from the town centre, and one in the huge square — reminiscent of St Mark's in Venice — which lies to the west of the Roman palace. Yet the inner city has kept its unique atmosphere.

Originally the settlement was in-shore on the landward side of a small rise, and a kilometre or two from the open sea. Here the city of Salona was built — originally called Aspalathos by the ancient Greeks. Salona was the birthplace of the Emperor Diocletian (AD 245–313) — born of Illyrian stock — whose army career led him on to becoming one of Rome's most powerful rulers (285–305). Diocletian was the only Roman emperor to 'retire' of his own free will and, to this end, he 'went back home to die', building his palace on the sea-front and even preparing his mausoleum.

The palace is vast, washed round by the sea on its southern side in those days, and with enough room for soldiers' quarters, granaries, temples and palace rooms for his family and for state visitors. Much of the palace is still there and, in about 614, when Salona was overrun and destroyed, the stricken inhabitants built their houses — indeed, their whole town — within the palace walls. Today, with the sea pushed back to make room for a wide promenade and many cafés and restaurants, the outer walls of the palace can be seen in perspective. The columns, arches and window openings look down across the road to the harbour, and the symmetry of this lovely palace still fills the beholder with awe. Through the arches, high up in the walls, medieval houses peer out between the columns. The way into the old city is still through Diocletian's gates. There are four of them — the Gold, Silver, Iron and Bronze or Copper gates — with the Golden Gate furthest from the sea and facing north, leading directly to Salona. Just outside this gate is the Meštrović statue of Bishop Grgur of Nin, many times life-sized. His big toe on one sandalled foot is polished bright by the touch of passers by: a way of 'touching wood', in memory of this valiant Croat cleric. On Marjan Hill, to the west of the palace, there is the Meštrović gallery in his post-war home which houses many of his works. He started life in Knin, not far away, by whittling carvings out of wood as a boy.

Museums are many in Split, with a wealth of Roman statuary and other remains, and there are frequent festivals, exhibitions, music festivals and drama performances. But it is still Diocletian and his palace that dominates the scene. Within

Diocletian's great palace still dominates the modern port of Split

174

the palace walls there are small squares, restaurants, an open-air market, shops and dwellings, all squeezed in with churches and the cathedral — once Diocletian's mausoleum. Then there is the peristyle which was the inner courtyard that gave direct access to the royal apartments. Not far away is the beautiful little temple of Jupiter. This exquisite building is perfectly preserved as, happily, it was made over into a baptistry. A good deal more of the palace has recently been excavated revealing basement halls and vast chambers — even the residual outlet from the imperial loo.

A 9 km aqueduct, its inner diameter 1 m wide, fed water to the palace. Part of this aqueduct can not only be seen on the road to Salona (modern Solin), but is still in use. The marks of history are everywhere, such as the tiny coffin of King Bela's daughter above the mausoleum portico. *Aida* has been performed, among the granite columns and the sphinx in the peristyle, before now.

It is not just the vastness of the royal home that stuns one, but the wonderful balance and perspective in the decoration of such a building. It exhibits all that first Greek, and then Rome's architects acquired and developed. No wonder Robert Adam came to Split — he knew it as Spalato — for his inspiration: you can see its influence round Edinburgh and London even today.

ZADAR

Zadar, which really marks the beginning of Dalmatia along the coast, is today a large waterfront town set at the edge of a fertile plain, protected by many off-shore islands. It has its own civil airport and a busy harbour at which the line ships and ferries call on their way up and down the Adriatic. The harbour is just outside the walls of the original medieval town which is built on a small peninsula. Zadar was known as Idassa in the fourth century BC but the Romans called it Jader or Jadera. Later it became part of Byzantium. Then the Franks overran it for a time but it was returned to Byzantine rule by the Treaty of Aachen in 812 AD. Not long afterwards it came under the jurisdiction of the Croat rulers, or Bans. Then in 1105 it recognised the sovereignty of King Koloman, the Hungaro/Croat ruler and from that time was often in conflict with Venice. One of its worst periods was in 1202 when the town was captured by the Crusaders who, on their way east and short of money, were cajoled by the Venetians into overrunning Zadar in return for a cash inflow. All these events have left Zadar with a passionate regard for freedom and a wealth of lovely buildings, plus massive city walls and gates emblazoned with the Lion of Venice when that power finally took over. Remarkably, within the walls the decumanus, the forum and other Roman remains are still visible.

The most imposing building, because of its great height and 'blind-arch' walls 27 m high, is the church of Sv Donat built at the side of the forum. This ninth-century church is circular and, being built on the paving slabs of the old forum, has no subterranean foundations. The builders adapted many of the huge stones left from Roman times, setting them upside down so that the carved inscriptions from pagan times, being reversed, could not invoke evil spirits.

Also close to the forum is the cathedral of St Anastasia which houses the saint's sarcophagus. Sadly, the sixth-century baptistry and font in the courtyard were destroyed by bombs during the last war. But the convent of St Mary and the monastery of St Francis, together with the church of St Simeon, escaped damage. The cathedral bell-tower was built in several stages and is remarkably tall. The highest section

St Donat's, Zadar, built on and with the remains of the vast Roman forum

Zadar's priceless gold and silver is now on permanent exhibition at St Mary's convent

was constructed by Thomas Jackson in 1892, and he modelled his part of it on the bell-tower of the cathedral on the island of Rab. This is the same Englishman, Sir Thomas Jackson, who wrote so delightfully about the Adriatic coast in the last century.

There are many treasures in Zadar but outstanding among them are the gold and silver exhibits recently arranged in St Mary's convent and now on permanent display. The nuns look after these priceless works of the goldsmith's art and take people round the quiet and beautifully lit rooms. Zadar has for many centuries been a centre for gold and silver smiths: a goldsmiths' guild was already established by 1176. But there is more to come. When you have been through the remarkable display of treasures in St Mary's, the nuns will quietly point you towards their church of St Simeon. For it is here on the high altar, that the town's most outstanding treasure rests. The church itself is gothic renaissance and baroque. There is often a service in progress with a choir of nuns but, when the church is quiet, it is possible to go up to the sarcophagus of St Simeon which was fashioned between 1377 and 1380. It weighs 250 kg and was commissioned by Queen Jelisava Kotromanić, wife of King Ludovic of Anjou and daughter of the Bosnian king Stjepan Kotromanić. On the coffin are scenes of St Simeon's life and historical details such as the entrance of King Ludovic to Zadar. The wooden coffin is covered inside and out with silver gilt and deeply embossed. The master goldsmith who created it was given 1,000 marks (about 240 kg) of silver to work with and paid 1,000 Florentine gold pieces to complete it within the year. In the event, his masterpiece took much longer.

Zadar has treasure and history, indeed. But like so many of these cities with their beginnings lost in time, it bristles with modern life and industry. Its tourism thrives, and so do its colourful markets. Being on flat ground, both the town and its surroundings are easy to explore; while a cultural visit can be eased by an interlude seated by the side of the forum, drinking at a café table. A walk along the Roman decumanus is enlivened by the boutiques that line it on either side.

Zadar remembers its troubled past as well as its triumphs and, though it still sports the Lion of Venice on its walls, it did not welcome the Italian occupation between the two world wars. Now, those troubles behind it, the town has expanded very fast.

C·H·A·P·T·E·R · 6
Practical Information

GETTING TO YUGOSLAVIA

There are twelve main international airports, as well as a number of smaller ones, in Yugoslavia and the vast majority of people visiting the country arrive by chartered or scheduled flights. Scheduled air services by JAT (Jugoslovenski Aero-transport) depart from London Heathrow every day of the week to Zagreb and Belgrade, with some extra direct flights to Ljubljana and Dubrovnik on certain days. They also fly direct from Manchester and Glasgow. Internal flights connect with the main airports within the country and are considerably less expensive than in most European countries. But for those people who prefer not to fly, there are several other easy ways of entering Yugoslavia.

Trains and long-distance scheduled coach services from London Victoria go to Zagreb for internal connections. Private cars can enter at any border point: yachts, too, so long as the correct papers are on hand, have no problems.

Every visitor needs a valid passport and, for some countries — including for example the United States and Eire — a visa is necessary though in many cases it is issued free. Tourists can also enter Yugoslavia by obtaining a 30-day tourist pass for a small fee, on production of an identity card or a valid passport.

ENTRY BY PRIVATE CAR

A Green Card insurance document is necessary for private cars entering the country. Failing this, it is possible to obtain Yugoslav insurance on entry at the frontier.

EUROPEAN FOOTPATHS (E6 YU)

Marked by a sign showing a man and a woman carrying rucksacks and alpine walking-sticks, the European long-distance footpath was opened in 1975. The trek, taking 12–14 days to cross Yugoslavia, leads across Europe from Denmark to Opatija.

YACHTS

There are 19 international ports of entry on the Yugoslav Adriatic coast and islands which are open throughout the year, plus six more which are open from 1 May until 31 October. The former are: Koper, Umag, Piran, Pula, Raša, Poreč, Rovinj, Rijeka, Mali Lošinj, Senj, Zadar, Šibenik, Metković, Split, Kardeljevo, Korčula, Dubrovnik, Herceg Novi, and Bar. The latter are: Izola, Novigrad, Primošten, Hvar, Kotor, and Budva. On docking at the nearest international port of entry, the master of the yacht must immediately contact the harbour master for a sailing permit, taking with him the appropriate documents i.e. sailing documents issued by the relevant foreign authority and documents certifying that the master and crew are competent to sail the vessel. Yugoslav sailing permits are valid for one year and allow unlimited navigation in Yugoslav waters and among the islands except in certain restricted areas where no sailing is permitted. A small chart can be obtained which clearly marks these few areas. In case of emergency or shipwreck, any harbour is open for a stricken vessel and its crew. Supplies are available in most ports, and in the larger ones — and in marinas — there are special refuelling installations.

FLOTILLA AND BARE BOAT SAILING

Besides the many private yachts sailing in Yugoslav waters, several companies operate flotilla sailing holidays and bare boat hire. A list of these can be obtained at the Yugoslav National Tourist Offices.

Marinas

There are now 19 fully equipped yacht marinas, and several more in preparation, from Izola near Trieste to Dubrovnik. Repairs and servicing can be carried out in most of them, and owners can leave their vessels to over-winter.

Tourist Tax

All visitors to Yugoslavia who come to the country as tourists must pay a small tax whether they are staying in hotels, camping sites, private accommodation or in their own boats. This is a tax per day which will be incorporated by tour operators into the cost of the holiday; for people travelling individually the tax is added on to the bill for accommodation.

Tourists staying in Yugoslavia with a valid passport — and a visa when applicable — can stay in the country for any period not exceeding three months. In special circumstances this period can be extended for a further three months (without the applicant leaving the country) by going to the local police station, filling in an application form, and paying a small tax.

Driving a Car in Yugoslavia

If you drive your own car in Yugoslavia you need only a valid driving licence and insurance papers which include either a Green Card or Yugoslav insurance cover. You must also display a country of registration plate, and it is quite useful to carry a spare GB plate, as children have been known to collect them! A red triangle must also be carried in case of emergency. A first aid box is obligatory for Yugoslav drivers, and all drivers are required to stop and render first aid if necessary.

Hiring a self-drive car entails producing a passport and valid driving licence.

In case of break-down, the Automobile Association of Yugoslavia (AMSJ) has a country-wide network; and the SPI is an on-the-road assistance unit for repairing and towing cars. It operates on major roads and towns throughout the country and can be reached by dialling 987. Most of the bigger garages in large towns can service most makes of foreign cars.

Accommodation

Except in July and August there is normally little need to book overnight accommodation in advance, unless you are in one of the most popular resorts. If you don't want an hotel room look for the sign 'SOBE' outside private homes. Private rooms are all inspected by local tourist authorities who also have lists of accommodation available. Rooms are graded according to comfort, and prices are very reasonable. Some housewives with rooms to let even meet the car-ferries, quietly calling out *sobe* — rooms?

Money

Foreign currency, travellers' cheques and Eurocheques can be exchanged for dinars at any bank, post office, exchange bureau or hotel that has an exchange office. The rate is fixed twice a week by the Bank of Yugoslavia and you get the same equivalent wherever you choose to change your money.

The bigger department stores often have a bank on the premises, and many of the larger shops accept credit cards in payment — also some restaurants.

Restaurant dining is not expensive in Yugoslavia and, curiously enough, is even more reasonable in Belgrade, the capital city, than it is along the coast. Except in some bigger hotels, it is possible to buy open carafe wine in restaurants reasonably priced and good. A bottled wine in an hotel will cost very much more than the equivalent in the supermarket, but hotels have to pay a heavy tax on their restaurant wines. Yugoslav wines, and their very good liqueurs and aperitifs, are much less expensive than imported equivalents.

Tipping

Although tipping is not obligatory, it is normal to add 10 per cent to bills.

Self Catering

There are mini and super markets everywhere in Yugoslavia making shopping without the language easy, though nearly all Yugoslavs having any contact with visitors speak some English: it is the No 1 foreign language taught in schools and most teenagers speak English surprisingly well. In the bigger food shops a number of pre-cooked dishes — both in tins and in foil — are available. There are also salamis and frozen foods. The fruit and vegetable markets are superb as well as colourful and the stalls are usually presided over by country-women — often in their village dress. The prices per kilo are usually scribbled on a card in the markets. The souvenir stalls don't usually display prices — whether it is for a beautiful ethnic rug, or a pair of wooden carved nut-crackers, etc — and it is often possible to bring down the price quite dramatically by a little judicious bargaining.

There is plenty of coffee and tea (though not the strong Indian variety) in Yugoslavia; both are expensive to buy and so make good small gifts if brought from home when you wish to show appreciation.

THE WATER

Yugoslavs drink a great deal of mineral water bottled in their many famous spas. But it is perfectly safe to drink the tap water throughout the country. Coming from mountain springs and underground rivers that flow through the limestone rock, it is extremely pure.

MEDICAL HELP

Medical help is given without charge to all foreign visitors whose countries have a reciprocal agreement. The only requirement is the production of your passport when first seeing the doctor. A small charge (very small by most standards) is made for drugs prescribed by the medical practitioner.

FISHING PERMITS

Fishing is possible on the many rivers, lakes and on the sea in Yugoslavia. The rivers in the mountains are rich in salmon, trout and grayling, etc. Permits are issued either by local authorities, fishing clubs or, in some cases, by local hotels. Fishing and underwater fishing is restricted to using certain equipment. No one may fish in marine nature reserves, ports, beaches or restricted zones. Information can be obtained locally.

CHURCHES

Although the three main religions in Yugoslavia are Roman Catholic, Serbian and Macedonian Orthodox, and Muslim, there are a few small Christian groups of other denominations. In Croatia, Slovenia and Dalmatia the churches are mostly Roman Catholic, with a few Orthodox and Protestant churches, and one or two synagogues. In the east of the country, that is to say in Montenegro, Serbia and Macedonia, the vast majority of the churches are Orthodox. There are still many working mosques in Bosnia, Serbia and Macedonia, as well as some in Montenegro. Visitors are welcome to worship in all the churches — including many attached to convents and monasteries.

THE TWO ALPHABETS

Nearly all public signs (street names, etc.) are now printed in the Latin alphabet, but in the eastern half of Yugoslavia the Cyrillic alphabet is the one in common use. So it can be a great help to know something of that alphabet, in case there is a problem. Then the word PECTOPAH, for example, holds the promise of a good meal as it is pronounced restaurant. Cyrillics are similar to Greek characters; anyone with a smattering of Greek — classical or otherwise — or Russian has no difficulty in reading it. And it does add to the enjoyment of a visit if you can read the local signs, albeit slowly!

NATIONAL PARKS

Yugoslavia is very proud of her natural heritage of scenic beauty and, in outstanding areas, has taken steps to protect the scenery, flora and fauna by designating them National Parks. This designation not only protects vast areas of unspoilt land, but some marine areas and life as well: for instance at Zavratnica Fjord, and the very beautiful and sheltered marine waters round the Kornat islands. Accommodation can usually be found in these National Parks. For botanists and marine biologists, these protected areas offer tremendous satisfaction.

SPAS

Health spas abound in Yugoslavia, and the clinics attached to each offer a great variety of treatment. Complete lists of the spas are available from the Yugoslav National Tourist Offices.

UNESCO

Ten places in Yugoslavia have been included in the official Unesco list of cultural and natural treasures of the world's heritage. These are: the towns of Dubrovnik, Split, Kotor and Ohrid; the monasteries of Sopočani and Studenica; the Plitvice and Ohrid lakes; Mount Durmitor; the Skocjan Caves.

THE LANGUAGE

There are three separate languages spoken in Yugoslavia, but all have the same Slav root. They are Slovenian, Macedonian and Serbo-Croat — a mixture of Serbian and Croatian where the main differences are variations in grammatical use and in a few of the words used. For example, the word for bread in Croatia is *kruh*, and in Serbia *hleb*. *Voz* and *vlak* both mean train; *paradiz* and *rajčica* both mean tomato, though in Dalmatia *pomodori* is often used.

Serbo-Croat is in official use (as are Slovenian and Macedonian), but even this varies from district to district according to whether the dialect is *e-kavski, je-kavski* or *ije-kavski*; the latter has a very liquid sound, less hard than in the other dialects. An example of this is the word for river, *reka*, which becomes *rijeka* in *ije-kavski*.

The pronunciation of the language is simpler than it looks if you follow a few basic rules. Every letter should be pronounced, so that the island of Krk, for instance, with all three letters stressed, sounds similar to a Scottish church! The letter 'J' takes the place of the letter 'Y' in Yugoslav (Jugoslav) and 'C' is pronounced like 'ts' — as in mats. There are two accents used to alter the pronunciation of a letter: these are ´ and ˇ. So that 'Ć' becomes tu, as in future, while 'Č' becomes ch, as in Charlie, or chat. 'Š' becomes sh, like shall or shut; 'Ž' becomes zh, like 'Jacques' in French. But, in fact, it is good enough just to insert an 'h' whenever you see an accent. Vowels never vary in the Yugoslav language; a is short, as in a north country 'mat'; e is short as in egg; i is pronounced like ee, as in sheet; o is short as in ox; but u is like oo as in shoot.

Yugoslavs are punctilious in their greetings. They always expect to shake hands, unless they know you very well in which case it can be a kiss on both cheeks — sometimes three times in Serbia! They will always pass the time of day, so it is pleasant, as well as very pleasing to them, to reciprocate. *Dobar Dan* for good morning or good day; *Dobro Veče* for good evening; *Laku Noč* for good night (literally easy or peaceful night). *Molim* is please — (*Prosim* in Slovenian); *Hvala* is thank you, and *Velika Hvala* if you wish to say Thank you very much. If you want to call a waiter's attention, call out *Molim* rather than *Konobar* (waiter), it sounds less peremptory! *Zdravo*! can be used for Hello; it really says 'Hail'. Goodbye is *Dovidjenja* (or *Nasvidanje* in Slovenian) but frequently these days, people are saying *Bog*, short for *Z' Bogom*, which means With God. If you wish to have or buy something, the verb *Voliti* means to want. But it can also be used as 'I love you', or I want you'; it is best to be forewarned!

Measurements

All measurements are given in metric units. For readers more familiar with the imperial system, the accompanying tables are designed to facilitate quick conversion to imperial units. Bold figures in the central columns can be read as either metric or imperial: e.g. 1 kg = 2.20 lb or 1 lb = 0.45 kg.

mm		in	cm		in	m		yds
25.1	1	.039	2.54	1	0.39	0.91	1	1.09
50.8	2	.079	5.08	2	0.79	1.83	2	2.19
76.2	3	.118	7.62	3	1.18	2.74	3	3.28
101.6	4	.157	10.16	4	1.57	3.66	4	4.37
127.0	5	.197	12.70	5	1.97	4.57	5	5.47
152.4	6	.236	15.24	6	2.36	5.49	6	6.56
177.8	7	.276	17.78	7	2.76	6.40	7	7.66
203.2	8	.315	20.32	8	3.15	7.32	8	8.75
228.6	9	.354	22.86	9	3.54	8.23	9	9.84

g		oz	kg		lb	km		miles
28.35	1	.04	0.45	1	2.20	1.61	1	0.62
56.70	2	.07	0.91	2	4.41	3.22	2	1.24
85.05	3	.11	1.36	3	6.61	4.83	3	1.86
113.40	4	.14	1.81	4	8.82	6.44	4	2.48
141.75	5	.18	2.27	5	11.02	8.05	5	3.11
170.10	6	.21	2.72	6	13.23	9.65	6	3.73
198.45	7	.25	3.18	7	15.43	11.26	7	4.35
226.80	8	.28	3.63	8	17.64	12.87	8	4.97
255.15	9	.32	4.08	9	19.84	14.48	9	5.59

ha		acres	Metric to imperial conversion formulae	
				multiply by
0.40	1	2.47		
0.81	2	4.97	cm to inches	0.3937
1.21	3	7.41	m to feet	3.281
1.62	4	9.88	m to yards	1.094
2.02	5	12.36	km to miles	0.6214
2.43	6	14.83	km^2 to square miles	0.3861
2.83	7	17.30	ha to acres	2.471
3.24	8	19.77	g to ounces	0.03527
3.64	9	22.24	kg to pounds	2.205

New Laws Passed in 1986

In line with its expansion of the tourist industry and other businesses, Yugoslavia has passed new laws regarding foreign investment in the country, and the leasehold and development of property. Until these new laws were passed, no foreign firm could invest more than 49 per cent of total capital involved, and the methods of remuneration and taxation were complicated, and sometimes prolonged. Now both difficulties have been considerably eased and simplified, and the restriction to less than half the total in foreign currency has been abolished. There must, however, be some proportion of Yugoslav investment, and a Yugoslav partner in any shared project.

Time-sharing is a new word in Yugoslavia, but the recently passed laws provide for individual time-sharing — of rooms, houses and apartments in Yugoslavia by foreigners for one or more weeks in each year for a period of between five and thirty years. The property can be sold, re-leased or transferred to another by the owner, or passed on as inheritance within the period of time stipulated. Foreign buyers of time-shared accommodation are liable for certain maintenance costs.

Foreign investment and joint ventures. Together with time-sharing, foreign tour operators and agencies can, in co-operation with Yugoslav partners, now lease land or property from Yugoslav owners, suitable for building tourist 'villages' or altering apartments, bungalows or houses for time-share leasing, during the period agreed on. At the end of that period the land and/or property will revert to the Yugoslav freehold owner, as is normal with leashold agreements. The agreement may, however, be re-negotiated for a further leasehold period.

So new and far reaching are these new laws and concepts that the details of how they will be interpreted are still, in 1987, being worked out. But the way does now seem clear for foreign investors in tourism to include Yugoslavia, with France, Spain and Italy, in their operations.

A LAND WITH SOMETHING FOR EVERYONE

Yugoslavia — one of the most beautiful countries in Europe, if not the world — has really come of age. Until 1945 she was predominantly agricultural, with little development of her extraordinarily rich and varied natural wealth. There was little education for the masses; and an underdeveloped social conscience among landowners. Now as a non-aligned nation she has emerged to play her full part in the world. There is medical care, and pensions for all; education is free for everyone. Her people take an intense interest in the rest of the world, and her main trouble at the present time is to maintain her balance of payments and curb inflation in such a free society. But there is always a warm welcome for foreign visitors of all nations. Yugoslavia — the country of seven frontiers, six republics, five nations, four main religions, three languages, and two alphabets — is these days one nation indeed.

Index

Aachen, Treaty of 175
Ada Island 52
Ada Summer Recreation Centre 151
Adam, Robert 175
Adriatic Sea 5
Aemona (see Ljubljana) 157
Aesop's *Fables* 20
Agenor, King 47
Agesilaus 87
Albania 5, 7, 93, 94, 96, 97
Aleutica 87
Alexander, King of Yugoslavia 50,128
Alexander the Great 93, 137
Amber Route 78, 139, 163
Anastasia 138
Andrić, Ivo 115, 119, 138
Ankaran 15
Apollonius 57
Argonauts 57
Arneri
    Family 81
    Palace 81
Arnerić (see Arneri) 81
Aspalathos 173
Athos, Mount 104, 106
Augustus, Emperor 47, 65, 169
Austria 7
Austrian Empire 7
Auto-route Zagreb/Belgrade 31
Avala, Mount 153
Avar Tribes 30, 37

Babino Polje 86, 88
Badija 84
Baikal Lake 137
Baka-Servis 3, 4
Balšić Family 47, 52
Baltic Sea 78
Banja Luka 31, 116, 118
Bar 50, 51
Barbat 66
Baščaršija 161
Baška 63, 65
Baška Stone 65
Baška Voda 27
Bassani 79
Beč (see Vienna)

Bela IV, King 23, 25, 68, 120, 175
Belgrade 5, 51, 97, 99, 109, 110,
    151–4
Bentinck 75
Beram 131
Betina 69
Bihač 119, 120
Biljarda 156
Biograd 18
Biokovo Mountains 28, 29
Biševo Island 55
Bitola 137, 159
Bjelašnica, Mount 145
Black Sea 5, 78, 151
Blandona 18
Blato 83
Bled, Lake and Town 145, 146, 147
Blue Grotto
    Biševo 76
    Mljet 87
Boeothia 47
Bogomil
    Graves 33, 155
    Heretic Religion 115, 116
Bogorodica 138
Bohinj 146–7
Bojana River 51, 52
Bol 72
Boris, Iguman 49
Bosnia 5, 6, 7, 21, 74, 78, 95,
    114–20
Bovec 148
Brač 4, 71–3
Brestova 60
Brioni Islands 4, 56, 57
British Military Mission to Marshal
    Tito 135
British R.M. Commandos Nos 40
    and 43 29, 73, 74
Brna 83
Budva Statute 48
Budva Town 3, 40, 43, 46, 47–8, 49, 55.
Buje 15
Bukhara 23
Bulgaria 7, 93, 94
Buna 31
Byzantium 8, 41, 47, 59, 94, 139

Cadmus 47
Calypso 87
Carpathian Mountains 8, 30, 37
Caska 67
Cavtat 37, 38, 88, 166
Caxton 155
Celje 128
Celts 119, 128
Central Asia 99
Ceremosnja Caves 110
Cetina River 27
Cetinje 45, 154–6
Chilander Monastery 106
Cividale 148
Colchis 52, 57, 58
Comes Marcilinus 162
Constantine, Emperor 99
Constantine Porphyrogenitus 17
Constantinople 8, 138
Cres
  Island 4, 16, 40, 57–60, 65
  Town 58
Crikvenica 16, 17, 63
Crna Gora 39 (see also
  Montenegro)
Crno Jezero 135, 136
Crnojević
  Dynasty 53, 155
Crnojević, Ivan 155
Croatia 7, 95, 118, 120–5
Croats 7
Crusaders 18, 175
Cyrillic Alphabet 8, 93, 137
Cyril, St 8, 93, 137, 159

Čakor Pass 98
Čara 82
Čele Kula 99
Čikat, Bay of 61
Čilipi 38
Čiovo Island 4, 23, 70
Čitluk 32

Dalmatia 7
Dalmatii 173
Dalmatinac, Juraj 68, 172
Dalmatinska Brigada 29
Dance of Death 130, 131
Danube River 5, 78, 93, 97, 110,
  111, 113, 126, 151
Dardanelles 140
Deakin, Col Sir William 29, 135
Dečani Monastery 49, 103
Despotovac 109
Dinaric Mountains 27, 60
Diocletian, Emperor 14, 70, 173

Dionysus 47
Djerdap 110
Djordje, Sv 42
Djordjević, Village and family 144
Dobričević Dobriža 20
Dobričević, Lovro 42
Dojran
  Lake 5, 93, 96, 140–2
  Town 140–1
Donja Brela 27, 28
Donji Milanovac 110, 111, 112
Drač (Durazzo) 137
Drače 89
Drava River 126, 127
Drim Rivers (Black Drim and White
  Drim) 136
Drina River 119
Drvenik Islands 4, 70
Dubrovnik 4, 5, 7, 34, 36, 43, 65, 86,
  166–9
Dubrovnik Airport (Čilipi) 38
Duchess of Windsor 81
Duff Cooper, Lady Diana 81
Dugi Otok, Island 4, 69
Dunav River (see R. Danube) 5,
  109, 151, 153
Durmitor, Mountain Range 5, 53,
  133–6, 147

Earthquake of 1979 41, 43, 48, 51
Edward VIII, King 81, 145
Elaphite Islands 88
Epidaurum 37
Epidaurus 37
Erasmus of Antioch 137, 160
Eugenija, Igumanija (see also
  Queen Milica) 102
Euphemia, St, church 15, 16
Euphemija, poetess 103
Euphrasius Basilica 14

Ferdinand, Archduke 7, 160
Fiume (see also Rijeka) 66, 170
Flowers, Island of 46
Foretić, Nikola 41
Frankopan family 63, 65, 120, 171
Fremantle, Admiral 22, 75
Fruška Gora 113

Gamzigrad 100
Genghis Khan 23, 120
George, Fort 75
Glagolitic script 16, 17, 60, 137
Golden Fleece 111

Golubac 109
Gornja Stubica 122
Greece 7, 93, 96
Grgur, Bishop 17, 174
Grocka 153
Gruž harbour and port 35
Gubec, Matija 123

Hajrudin, architect 32
Haludovo 63
Hapsburgs 7, 32, 61, 114, 171
Hektorović, Petar 79
Heraclea Lincestis 139
Herceg Novi 40, 41
Hercegovina 6, 7
Homo Crapiensis 122
Homolje Mountain 110
Hope, Cape of Good 61
Hoste, Capt William 22, 75
Hrastovlje 130
Hum, Mount 75
Hungary 7
Hvar Island 4, 40, 65, 72, 73, 77–80
    Town 77–8
Hypnos, god 42

Ibar River 103, 106
Igalo 41
Igman, Mount 145
Ilidža 161
Illyrian Provinces 22, 157
    Tribes 40
Ilovik Island 58, 61
Imotski 28
Ingoli, Matteus 27
Iris Dalmatinus 89
Iron Gates Gorge 109, 111
Istanbul 99, 102, 137
Istrian Peninsula 2, 13, 16
Italy 7

Jackson, Sir Thomas 176–7
Jadrolinija Shipping Line 86
Jahorina, Mount 144
Jajce 31, 116, 117, 118, 120
Jason 57, 58, 111
Jaz 46
Jedera (see also Zadar) 21
Jelsa 79
Jeruzalem 127
John, Knights of St 41
Julian Alps 5
Julius Caesar 125
Jurandvor 65
Justinian 162

Kačić, family 27
Kairos, god 23, 24
Kalemegdan 151
Kaliste 138
Kamenari 41
Kanin, Mount 148
Karadjordje dynasty 153
Karadjordjevic, Petar, King of
    Serbia 102
Karavanke Alps 5
Kardeljevo 31
Karlovac, Treaty of 95
Kastav 171
Kaštelanski Žaljiv 24
Kavadarci 96
Klek 34
Kliment, St 8, 93, 137, 159, 160
Klis 25, 26, 71, 115
Knež 84
Kneža 85
Knights Templars 20
Knin 174
Koch, Dr Robert 57
Koločep Island 4, 88
Koloman, King 18, 175
Komiža 74, 75
Konavli 38, 39
Konovoski Dvoru 39
Kopaonik 5, 143–4
Koper 15, 130
Koran, the 97
Korčula Island 4, 30, 40, 41, 55, 65,
    71, 73, 76, 80–6, 90, 91
    Town 80–2, 84
Korkyra Melaina 82
Kornat Islands 68
Kosovo 51, 97, 98
Kosovo Polje 49, 95, 100, 102, 103,
    152
Kotor
    Fjord 40, 48, 156
    Town 41, 42, 43, 45
Kotromanić, Jelislava, Queen 177
    Stjepan, King 177
Kovačica 114
Kragujevac 100, 108, 109
Kraljevica 16, 63
Kraljevo 100, 102, 103, 104, 106
Kranjska Gora 147–8
Krapanj Island 70
Krapina 121, 122
Krapinske Toplice 121
Krapinski Čovjek, (see Homo
    Crapiensis) 122
Kratovo 97
Krešimir, King Peter 18, 68, 172

Krk
  Airport 63
  Island 4, 16, 62–5
  Town 63–4, 65
Krka River (Croatia) 18, 69
  Falls 18
Krka River (Slovenia) 128
Kruševac 100, 102
Kučevo 111
Kugij, Dr J 149
Kumrovec 121
Kupari 36, 37
Kurbinovo 139
Kvarner Bay 16, 57, 58, 170

Labin 16
Lastovo
  Island 4, 20, 56, 73, 76–7
  Town 76
Lazar, King 100, 102
Lazarica 109
Lepenski Vir 111, 112
Lepetane 41, 42
Leš (Albania) 136
Lesnovo 97
Liburnija 17
Lichnidos (see also Ohrid) 136, 137, 158
Lilium Buthuense 55
Lim Fjord 15
Lipica 5, 129, 130
Lippizaner horses 5, 57, 129
Ljubljana 126, 157–8
Ljubljanica River 157, 158
Ljubljanska Vrata 157
Ljubostinija 102, 103, 109
Lokrum Island 88, 169
Lopud Island 4, 88
Lošinj Island 58, 60–1, 65
Lovčen, Mount 45
Lovište 90, 91
Lovren 171
Lowen, Col Peter 82
Lučica, Bay of 50
Ludvic, King of Anjou 177
Lumbarda 84
Lun 68

Macedonia 7, 93–7, 115
Maclean, Brigadier Sir Fitzroy 135
Maglić (fortress) 106
Majdanpek 110, 111
Makarska 3, 27, 28, 29
Mali Lošinj 60, 61
Mali Rat 27
Mali Ston 34, 35
Manasija Monastery 109

Marco Polo 86
Maribor 125–7
Maria Theresa 127
Marija Bistrica 124
Marina 22
Marko Sv, Island 45
Marmont, General 24
Maximilian, Emperor of Mexico 88
Medea 57
Mediana 99
Medjugorje 124
Medović, Celestin 79
Medulin 16
Melita, (see Mljet) 86
Meštrović, Ivan 152, 153, 172, 174
Metajna 68
Methodius, St 8, 93, 137, 159
Milena, Queen 45
Milica, Queen 49, 100, 102, 103
Miljačka River 161
Mithras 118
Mlini 37
Mljet, Island 4, 86–8, 90
Mongolian Hordes 23
Montenegro 3, 6, 7, 39–53, 95, 97
Moore, Henry 83
Morača Monastery, (fresco) 105
Morava River 99, 109
Moravica River 100
Moreška Sword Pageant 86
Morinj 42
Morlachs (see Vlachs)
Moščenice 171
Moščenićka Draga 16, 171
Mostar 31, 32, 33, 116, 124
Motovun 15
Murex 3
Murter 4, 69

Nagovičano 97
Napoleonic Era 82
Naum, St 8, 93, 137, 138
Nelson, Admiral Horatio 22
Nemanja dynasty 95, 104
Neretva River 5, 30, 31, 78
Nerežišća 73
Nero, Emperor 47
Neum 33, 34
Nikola, King of Montenegro 40, 45, 154, 156
Nin, 17
Niš 99, 144
Njegoš
  Danilo 155, 156
  dynasty 155
  Petar Petrović II 154, 155, 156

Njeguši 156
Njivice 63
Novalja 67, 68
Novi Dojran 141
Novigrad 17
Novi Sad 112, 113, 114
Novi Vinodolski 16
Novo Mesto 128

Obod Printing Press 53, 155
Ogadai 23, 68
Ohrid Lake 5, 93, 96, 136–8
  Town 104, 137, 158–60
Olympias 93
Omiš 27, 71
Omišalj 63
Opatija 16, 170–I
Oplenac, Mount 153
Orašac 36
Orebić 80, 90, 91
Orlando Statue 36, 37
Oršić family 122, 164
Osor 57
Ostrogoths 41
Otočec 128
Otranto, Bay of 51
Ottoman Empire 7, 26

Pag Island 4, 17, 65, 67–8
  Town 68
Pakleni Islands 78
Palma, the Younger 27
Palmer, A.W. 141
Pannonian Plain 114, 164
Papava Somniferom 94, 95
Pašman Island 69
Pastrović family 49
Paul, St 87
Pazin 15, 131
Peasants' Revolt 123
Pek River 110, 111
Pelješac Peninsula 30, 31, 34, 55,
  73, 80, 86, 188–91
Perast 42, 43
Persia 99
Peter, the Great of Russia 43
Petračane 18
Petrovaradin 113, 114
Petrovac 40, 50
Philip of Macedon 93, 127, 137
Phoenix Canariensis 76
Piran 15
Pirot 99
Plat 37
Pliny 47
Plitvice Lakes 5, 124–5
Pliva River 117

Plivska Lakes 119
Ploče (see also Kardeljevo) 31
Počitelj 31
Podgora 27, 29
Pogradec 137
Pohorje Mountain 127
Polače 86, 87, 90
Pomine 86, 87
Poreč 2, 3, 13
Porozina 60
Portorož 2, 15
Postojns 128
Potomje 89
Praskvica Monastery 48, 49
Preko 69
Prespa Lake 5, 96, 136, 138–9
Prevlaka 46
Prilep 96
Primošten 21, 70
Prince Bishops 155
Princip, Gavrilo 160
Priština 97
Prižba 83
Prizren 97
Proteus Anguinus 120
Pseudoskylax 71
Ptuj 127–8
Pula 4, 13, 16, 57, 169–70
Punat 64
Punta Križa 58
Pupnat 82

Rab Island 4, 65–7, 68
Rabac 13, 16
Račišće 85
Radovan 24
Ragusa (see Dubrovnik)
Rapallo, Treaty of 67, 170
Religions 7
Resava (see Manasija) 109
Resava River 109
Resavska Pečina 109
Richard, King, the Lionheart 169
Rijeka 16, 60, 67, 170–1
Rijeka Črnojevića 53, 155
Rječina River 170
Risan 41, 42
Robertson, Fort 75
Rogač 71
Rogoznica 22
Roman Empire 8
Romania 7, 109, 110
Rovinj 13, 15, 16
Rugovo Canyon 98
Ruma 113
Russia 93

Salona 24, 71, 173, 175
Salonika 93, 94, 137, 140
Samarkand 23
Samuilo, King 139, 159
Saracens 59
Sarajevo 7, 31, 116, 144–5, 160–1
Sava River 5, 95, 97, 120, 126, 147, 151, 164
Sava, St 104, 106
Savica Falls 147
Savina Monastery 41
Scutari (see Skadar) 52, 53
Senj 16, 26, 61, 63, 65, 115
Septimus Severus 87
Serbia 7, 93, 95, 97–114
Serbs 7
Serbs, Croats and Slovenes, Kingdom of 6
Shaw, G.B. 57, 171
Shells 3, 29
Simeon, King 139
Simeon, St, Myrobliptos (see Stefan Nemanja) 106
Simpson, Wallis (see Duchess of Windsor) 81
Sinj 26, 27
Sinjska Alka 26
Skadar, Lake 5, 48, 51, 52, 155
Skadarlija 153
Skofja Loka 128
Skopje 94, 95, 96, 161–3
Skylax 47
Slavonia 95
Sljeme 165
Slovenia 2, 7, 125–31
Slovenska Bistrica 127
Smokvica 82
Soča River Valley 148, 149
Socialist Republic of Yugoslavia 118
Socrates 47
Sokobanja 99, 100, 104, 106
Solaris 18
Solin 71, 175
South Adriatic United Nations Plan 2
Spalato (see also Split) 175
Split 4, 5, 22, 65, 71, 72, 74, 75, 115, 173–5
Srebreno 37
Stalin 8
Stari Grad 78
Statenburg Schloss 127
Stečci 22
Stefan, Despot 109
Stefan Dušan 95, 140, 141

Stefan, son of King Lazar 103
Stefan Nemanja 47, 104, 106, 155
Stefan Prvovenčani (First-Crowned) 104, 107
Stjepan Tvrtko 32, 161
Stobi 96
Stolac 116
Ston 34
Struga 137, 138
Strumica 96
Stuart, Capt. William 29, 135
Stubičke Toplice 122
Studenica 98, 106, 107
Suleiman II 97
Supetar 73
Susak 58, 61–2
Sušak 170
Sutjeska 135
Sutomore 50
Sveti Ilija, Mount 90
Sveti Stefan 46, 48, 49

Šar Mountains 96
Šibenik, 4, 18, 21, 68, 69, 70, 171–3
Šilo 63
Šipan 88
Škrpjela, Gospa od 42
Šolta 4, 71
Štip 96, 97
Šubić family 25, 27
Šumarice Memorial Park 108

Tajna Večera 80, 107
Tanganyika, Lake 137
Tara Canyon 134
Tara River 133
Tarvisio 148
Telephose, Queen 47
Tetovo 96
Teuta, Queen 41
Thebes 47
Theodosius 47
Thessaloniki (see Salonika), 140
Tiberius, Emperor 109
Time Sharing 11, 187
Titian 79
Tito, President 4, 8, 29, 41, 50, 56, 75, 89, 118, 121, 135, 146, 153
Titograd 154
Titov Veles 96
Tivat 45
Tomašević, Stjepan, King 118
Tomislav, King 17, 18, 25
Topkapi Palace 102
Topola 153
Trajan's Tablet 109, 110

Travnik 118, 119
Trebenište 137
Trebinje 39
Trento 149
Trifun, Sv, Cathedral 44
Triglav, Mount 5, 147, 148
Trogir 22, 23, 24, 70
Trpanj 89
Trsat 170–1
Trstenik 86, 89, 90
Trsteno 35
Tučepi 27, 28, 29

Ubli 76, 77
Učka, Mount 171
Ugljan Island 4, 69
Ulcinj 43, 51, 52
Ulus Ali 52
Ulysses 87
Umag 13
Una River 120
Unesco 43, 135
United Nations 2
Uskok Pirate Heroes 61, 115
Uvala Scot 171

Valun Stone 60
Vardar River 96, 162, 163
Vauban, Military architect 114
Vela Luka 80, 82, 83
Vela Špilja 83
Velebit Mountains 59, 67
Veli Lošinj 60, 61
Veli Rat 27
Veneziano, Paolo 65
Verige Bay 56
Veronese, Paulo 79
Via Egnatia 137, 138, 139
Victory, Spirit of 152
Vidova Gora 72
Vienna 95, 129
Villach 148
Vinodol Code 16, 170
Vintgar Falls 146
Vir Pazar 51, 53
Vis Island 4, 40, 55, 56, 73, 74–6
    Town 74, 75
Višegrad 119

Visovac 20
Vlachs 155
Vladika 155
Vlaho, Sv 168
Vodice 18
Vogel, Mount 147
Vojvodina 97, 112, 113, 114
Vrana, Lake (Croatian mainland)
    20
    Lake (on Island Cres) 59
    Village (Cres Island) 59
    Village (Mainland Croatia) 20, 21
Vranjina, Island 53
Vrbas River 116, 117
Vrbnik 65
Vrboska 79
Vrnačka Banja 104, 106
Vrnik Island 71, 84
Vrsar 15
Vršić 147
Vrtić 4
Vuk, son of King Lazar 103
Vukčić-Hrvatinić, Hrvoje 117, 118,
    120

Wellington, Fort 75
West, Rebecca 81

Zadar 4, 5, 17, 18, 21, 59, 60, 65, 68,
    69, 172, 175–8
Zagorje 121, 122
Zagreb 95, 120, 163–6
Zaječar 100
Zaton (near Šibenik) 36
    Mali 35
    Veli 35
Zeta 47, 155
Zlarin 69, 70
Zlatni Rat 72, 73
Zrinski family 164
Zvonimir, King 65
Žabljak 5, 53, 133, 135
Žabljak Castle 53
Ženska Plaža 52
Žiča, Monastery 103, 104, 106
Žrnovo 82, 83
Žuljana 90
Župa, Bay of 36, 37, 38, 88